Personality

PERSONALITY

Measurement and theory

Paul Kline
Reader in Psychology, University of Exeter

St. Martin's Press   New York

ISBN 0–312–60230–8

Library of Congress Cataloging in Publication Data
Kline, Paul.
  Personality: measurement and theory.
  Bibliography: p.
  Includes index.
  1. Personality assessment. 2. Personality tests.
3. Personality. I. Title.
BF698.4.K56 1983b   155.2′8   83–13798
ISBN 0–312–60230–8

Contents

1 General problems in psychological measurement

If we are to arrive at a scientific understanding of personality based upon measurement, it is clear that our measures of personality must be at least adequate. Before we can discuss the manifold problems of personality measurement it is necessary first to deal with more general problems of psychological measurement, for it is in the light of these that personality measurement can be assessed.

The use of scales

The aim of measurement is to produce an accurate score on some variable. To take an example from personality, we might want to measure anxiety. In clinically based theories of personality, such as psychoanalysis, anxiety is highly important. Clinicians regularly describe their patients as 'unanxious' or 'highly anxious'. Such descriptions imply measurement. The aim of a quantified, scientific psychology of personality is to make such implicit measurement explicit and precise. In attempting to measure anxiety, a number of different scales or scaling procedures can be used.

Nominal scales

In nominal scales subjects are classified into different categories with no implication of the quantitative relationships between them: typical examples are male/female or socialist/conservative. This is a highly primitive form of measurement, creating only two groups. It is to be noted, however, that even in the discrete categories of our examples an underlying continuum may be discerned. Thus, males and females can be seen as the poles of the male–female continuum, the population being bimodally distributed. Similarly, conservatives and socialists could be seen as lying on a dimension of liberalism. Obviously, nominal scales have little place in psychological measurement.

Ordinal scales

In ordinal scales, as the name suggests, subjects are ranked on the variable being measured. Since ranking implies that we do not know the units of the measuring scale, an ordinal scale is again (as with nominal scales) a primitive form of scaling.

Interval scales

In interval scales all differences of the same size at any point in the scale have the same meaning. For example, in the old-fashioned method of assessing the intelligence quotient, the measured mental age was divided by chronological age and multiplied by a hundred. The problem with this kind of scaling should be clear, and it illustrates the importance of interval scaling. Thus an 8-year-old child has a mental age of 10. This gives him an IQ of $\frac{10}{8} \times 100 = 125$. However, a 12-year-old child with a mental age of 14 has an IQ of $\frac{14}{12} \times 100 = 117$. Now, in each case an improvement of two years in respect of mental age over chronological age results in different intelligence quotients. The point is that, rightly or wrongly, the scale of measurement has intervals of unequal meaning at different points in the scale. This fact clearly makes the interpretation of scales with unequal intervals difficult and statistical analysis meaningless. Interval scales, however, allow of statistical analysis and comparison between different scales and hence are a minimum requirement for psychological measurement.

Ratio scales

Ratio scales are interval scales with a meaningful zero. Although this point may be hard to conceptualize for many psychological variables, there are methods of test construction which enable ratio scales to be constructed, and these will be discussed below in appropriate chapters.

Clearly, therefore, it can be seen that good psychological testing (indeed, any form of measurement) demands at least interval scales and, ideally, ratio scales. Many tests yield scores which have never been shown to fit our definition of an interval scale. Generally, this is simply assumed, and if sensible results can be demonstrated using the test on the assumption that it is an interval scale, then it is arguable that such presumptions are tenable.

From the viewpoint of the measurements of personality, we must demand from our tests that they yield scores that are either ratio or interval scales or can reasonably be assumed to be such.

Psychological tests must be reliable, valid and discriminating.

Test reliability

In psychometrics reliability has two meanings. A test is said to be reliable if it is self-consistent. It is also said to be reliable if, on retesting, it yields the same score for each subject (given that subjects have not changed). This reliability over time is known as 'test–retest reliability'.

If we are assessing the merits of a test – as we well might in evaluating research reports, designing research or carrying out psychological testing in an educational, clinical or industrial setting – it is essential to ascertain whether a test is reliable. To do this it is necessary to know how reliability is measured and to be acquainted with the problems associated with such measurement.

Measuring internal consistency reliability

Split-half reliability The simplest measure of the internal consistency of a test is the split-half reliability. As the name suggests, half the test is correlated with the other half. The split can be by order of items – the first twenty with the last twenty or, in the case of ability tests in which the later, more difficult items may not be attempted by all subjects, odd items with even items.

Split-half reliability is a reasonably accurate measure of internal consistency, although how the test is split must obviously affect the results to some extent. A reliability coefficient of 0.7 or larger is necessary (for reasons to be discussed below) for a test to be considered satisfactorily consistent.

In evaluating split-half reliability coefficients two points must be noted, both concerning the samples from which the figures have been obtained.

1 Ideally, the reliability coefficients must be derived from samples similar to those on which the test is used or to be used. For

example, if an anxiety test has a reliability of 0.8 with a normal population, there is no guarantee that such a figure will be accurate for psychiatric patients or criminal offenders. Separate coefficients should be quoted for different populations.

2   The sample from which the coefficient has been obtained should be sufficiently large to make the figures statistically reliable. In practice, this means minimum sample sizes of about 100 subjects.

The alpha coefficient (Cronbach, 1951)   This is regarded by psychometrists (e.g. Nunnally, 1978) as the most efficient method of measuring the internal consistency of a test. In effect, coefficient alpha indicates the average intercorrelation between the test items and any set of items drawn from the same domain (i.e. items measuring the same variable). Coefficient alpha increases as the intercorrelations between the test items rise, a fact of some importance in evaluating the meaning of alpha reliability, as we discuss below in the section on the importance of internal consistency reliability.

KR20 reliability (Richardson and Kuder, 1939)   This is a special form of the alpha coefficient adapted for use with dichotomous items. Since many personality inventories use such dichotomous items (of the yes/no or true/false variety), this index is frequently to be found in the study of personality tests.

These are the main methods used in the computation of internal consistency reliability. As was the case with split-half reliability, both the alpha coefficient and KR20 need to be derived from samples of adequate size and constitution.

Occasionally, two other methods of computing the internal consistency of a test can be found in the research literature.

The factor-analytic method   If a test is factor analysed along with a variety of other tests, the square of its factor loadings can be shown (e.g. Guilford, 1956) to be its reliability. This is a powerful method of computing reliability. However, in evaluating this coefficient, it must be borne in mind that its actual value depends considerably on the particular tests with which a test has been factored and the technical adequacy of the factor analysis. Unless there are good grounds (and there rarely are) for arguing that there has been a proper sampling of test variables and of subjects, and that the factor analysis is sound, then any figures must be treated with caution.

Hoyt's (1941) analysis of variance method In this approach test variance is broken down into two sources – item and subjects (together, of course, with their interaction). The smaller the variance due to items, the higher the reliability of the test.

The present author (Kline, 1971; Kline, 1980b), in developing three personality tests, Ai3Q, OOQ and OPQ, has found little practical difference in any of these indices. Generally, however, Cronbach's alpha coefficient is the most efficient, being independent of any particular split of the test.

The meaning and importance of internal consistency reliability

Psychometrists are eager to develop tests which are highly self-consistent for the obvious reason that if part of a test is measuring a variable, then the other parts, if not consistent with it, cannot be measuring that same variable. Thus from this argument it would appear that for a test to be valid (i.e. for it to measure what it claims to measure), it *must* be consistent: hence the psychometric emphasis on internal consistency reliability. Indeed, the general psychometric view is exactly this, that high reliability is a prerequisite of reliability (e.g. Guilford, 1956; Nunnally, 1978). The only dissenting voice of any note is that of Cattell (e.g. Cattell and Kline, 1977). Cattell argues that high internal consistency is actually antithetical to validity on the grounds that any item must cover less ground or must be narrower than the criterion we are trying to measure. Thus if all items are highly consistent, they are also highly correlated, and hence a reliable test will measure only a narrow variable of little variance. As support for this argument it must be noted (a) that it is true that Cronbach's alpha increases with the item intercorrelations and (b) that in any multivariate predictive study the maximum multiple correlation between tests and the criterion (in the case of tests, items and the total score) is obtained when the variables are uncorrelated. This is obviously so, in that if two variables were perfectly correlated, one would be providing no new information. Thus maximum validity, in Cattell's argument, is obtained with test items that correlate not all with each other but each positively with the criterion. Such a test would have only low internal consistency reliability. Theoretically Cattell is correct in our view. However, to our knowledge no test constructor has managed to write items that, while correlating with the criterion, do not correlate with each other. Barrett and Kline (1982) have examined Cattell's own personality test, the 16PF test fully discussed on p. 52, in which such an attempt has been made, though it appears not to be entirely successful.

In the case particularly of personality questionnaires, high reliability should be treated with caution, since by writing items that are virtually paraphrases of each other high coefficients can be obtained, but at the expense of validity. Despite these comments, generally the psychometric claim holds: in practice, valid tests are highly consistent.

Test–retest reliability

Measurement   The measurement of test–retest reliability is simple. All that is required is the correlation of test scores on two occasions. To be useful, tests should have a test–retest reliability of at least 0.7. Concerning the necessity of higher test–retest reliability, for good psychological tests there is no dispute. However, a few points have to be watched in evaluating this aspect of a test.

1   As was the case with internal consistency reliability, the sampling must be sound (i.e. sample size should be not less than 100 subjects, and these should constitute a representative group).
2   The interval between testing sessions should be not less than a month, since a shorter interval than this may produce a spuriously inflated figure if subjects remember their previous responses.
3   To overcome this difficulty, some tests are constructed with parallel forms. In this case subjects take a different set of items on each occasion and test–retest reliability becomes parallel-form reliability. Where parallel forms of tests exist, there are considerable problems in demonstrating that the tests are properly parallel. Even if the correlation between the forms is high, this does not entirely meet the criterion of comparability, since to be truly parallel each equivalent item in the two tests should be shown to have the same response split in different populations and the same correlations with other scores. This is almost impossible to achieve. However, high parallel-form reliability probably permits the two tests to be interchanged in research with groups. For individual use, however, this writer is more sceptical.
4   Some good psychological tests can have low test–retest reliability if it can be argued that over time the variable is likely to have changed non-systematically among individuals, as is the case, for example, with measures of mood.

Generally, however, it is obvious that if tests are to be valid, they should yield the same score for individuals on any occasion; hence high test–retest reliability is a prerequisite of any sound test.

Test validity

The importance of reliability *per se* is small (other than for theoretical psychometrics): the emphasis on it arises from the fact that, as we have seen, high validity usually requires high reliability.

A test is said to be valid if it measures what it purports to measure. Such a definition is not as banal as it first appears, for two reasons: (a) the majority of tests, especially personality tests, are not valid, as even a brief perusal of the authoritative test reviews to be found in Buros's *Mental Measurement Yearbooks* (e.g. Buros, 1978) will show; (b) the demonstration of validity, again particularly for personality tests, is exceedingly difficult.

There are logical problems in the demonstration of test validity that have to be understood if tests are to be properly used, especially for the construction of theory. These, however, are best explicated after we have scrutinized the different kinds of validity to be found in discussions of tests.

Types of validity

Face validity Face validity receives a mention only to be dismissed. A test is face-valid if it appears to measure what it claims to measure. Such an appearance can be quite misleading, and face validity is unrelated to true validity. It is important only because absurd tests, for example, may induce unco-operative attitudes in subjects taking them. Hence face validity is useful in establishing good rapport and co-operation. It is also important to realize that a personality questionnaire cannot be evaluated through an examination of the content of its items (i.e. its face validity).

Concurrent validity Concurrent validity is assessed by correlating a test with other measures given at the time. Thus if we are attempting to measure anxiety, the concurrent validity of the test will be derived from its correlations with other of anxiety and other measures. This example illustrates the logical problems inherent in concurrent validity.

1 If the test correlates highly with other measures of anxiety, the question arises of whether these tests are themselves valid. If they are, a new question is proposed: what does the new test offer? If they are not valid, there is little point in attempting to discover their correlations with the new test.

2 If the test does not correlate at all with tests which are not designed to measure anxiety, then certainly this is some support for its validity, for, as with definitions, as Socrates stressed, it is important to state what the test is not measuring. However, on its own this is not sufficient. For while, if valid, a test of anxiety would not correlate with extraversion, mathematical ability and interest in cars, the same would also be true of a valid measure of psychoticism.

In brief, the problem with concurrent validity studies lies in establishing adequate criteria.

Predictive validity   A test may be said to possess predictive validity if it is able to predict some criterion score. To establish the predictive validity of an anxiety test, for example, we could follow up the subjects and see whether there were any correlation between scores on the test and subsequent admission to a psychiatric hospital or subsequent treatment for non-medical complaints.

If a test is able to predict in this way, this is impressive support for its validity. Again, the difficulty of establishing the predictive validity of most tests resides in setting up a predictive study (i.e. in finding a convincing criterion). However, if this can be done, predictive validity can be a useful method of demonstrating test validity.

Suffice it to say that with both concurrent and predictive validity studies sampling must be representative, and the numbers of subjects used must be large enough to allow for generalization.

Construct validity   Cronbach and Meehl (1955) developed the notion of construct validity, which is particularly useful for personality tests, for which it is usually difficult to find adequate criteria. For construct validity a large number of hypotheses are formulated concerning the test scores – hypotheses derived from the nature of the variable as a psychological construct. These hypotheses frequently involve both concurrent and predictive validity studies. The test may be said to have construct validity or not depending upon the overall set of results. We shall exemplify the method using a hypothetical anxiety test.

1 High scorers will be more likely to attend psychiatric clinics than low scorers.
2 High scorers will be more likely to be prescribed psychotropic drugs than low scorers.
3 The children of high scorers will score more highly on anxiety tests than the children of low scorers (there is both a hereditary and an environmental component in the determination of these scores – see Eysenck, 1967).
4 The anxiety test will correlate highly and significantly (beyond 0.6) with other tests of trait anxiety.
5 The anxiety test will not correlate with variables unconnected with anxiety.
6 Psychiatric groups characterized as anxious will score more highly than controls on the test.
7 On the test of anxiety subjects rated by supervisors and colleagues as anxious will score more highly than those rated non-anxious.

If all these seven hypotheses were to be supported, then it would be difficult to argue that the test was not measuring anxiety.

The main difficulty with the establishment of construct validity for a test resides in the fact that ultimately it is subjective rather than objective, whether or not the test is valid. In the hands of clever psychometrists, it can be argued, almost any set of results can be made to attest to validity. This means that the rationale of the hypotheses must be clearly stated. Despite this problem, for personality tests, where it is difficult to use a single criterion with any confidence, construct validity is the best approach to validity. Psychologists must evaluate critically construct studies before accepting or rejecting a test as valid or invalid.

Finally, as should be obvious from our examples, validity cannot be reduced to a single coefficient, unlike reliability. It makes no sense to claim that the validity of a test is 0.8. With every kind of validity, the evidence must be carefully scrutinized.

Although there are other methods in psychometrics for measuring validity, we shall leave these out of our discussion, since in the main those most appropriate for personality tests have been examined and described.

From our discussion so far it is clear that a good psychological test must be reasonably consistent, reliable over time and of demonstrated validity. In addition, it should be discriminating.

Test discrimination

Ferguson (1949) has developed an index of discriminability, Δ (delta), which runs like a correlation from 1 downwards – 1 being the maximum possible discrimination as shown by a rectangular distribution: for a normal distribution Δ is 0.92. In brief, therefore, we can see why the requirements of good psychological tests are summarized as reliability, validity and discrimination. Despite the problems of measuring reliability and demonstrating validity, which we have fully discussed, there is usually little doubt which tests meet standards that are by no means rigorous.

Before leaving the topic of reliability and validity, we shall outline briefly the model of measurement implicit in the above discussion. Even a slight acquaintance with the model will illuminate the nature of personality testing.

The classical model of error measurement

This classical measurement model has been fully described by Nunnally (1978), its descriptive title being derived from the fact that it has underlain psychological testing from its infancy. Even though recently more sophisticated models have been produced, these by no means outmode the classical theory, which is simple and can still be shown to be effective.

We shall first define two essential terms.

In the classical model an assumption is made that each individual for any trait (e.g. anxiety or extraversion) has a *true score*. The actual score a subject obtains on a test, the fallible score, differs from the true score due to random error. From this assumption it follows that if we test a subject repeatedly, a distribution of scores around his true score will result. The mean of this distribution, which is assumed to be normal, approximates the true score.

The classical model of error further assumes that any test consists of a random sample of items from the *universe of items* measuring the particular trait. In the case of personality tests such a universe of items is hypothetical, although in certain tests (e.g. of vocabulary or musical notation) the universe is finite.

Although in most tests items are not in reality selected randomly, Nunnally (1978) argues that the very diversity of items in most tests allows the assumption of randomness to be made. Error in tests arises from the fact that to a varying extent items do not reflect the item universe, and the more they fail to do so, the greater the error.

The true score is the score a subject would obtain if he were given all items in the item universe. Thus test error reflects the extent to which the test items accurately sample this item universe.

Statistical assumptions and basis of the classical model

In this book it would not be appropriate to set out the complete statistical basis of the classical model, although from it are derived many of the most important psychometric principles. For this readers must be referred to a brilliant exposition by Nunnally (1978), which in any case forms the basis of our summary.

Obviously, the notional universe of items will yield a notional matrix of inter-item correlations. The average inter-item correlation $\bar{r}_{i,j}$ indicates the size of the core common to all items in the universe. A collection of unrelated items would have an $\bar{r}_{i,j}$ of 0.00, indicating that they had nothing in common. In the model it is assumed that each item shares the common core equally with all others. From this it follows that in the model the average correlation of each item with all others is the same for each item. This is the basic assumption of the classical model, and from it can be derived a number of important psychometric points, as Nunnally (1978) shows.

Before listing these one important aspect of the model must be stressed. For personality tests especially, in which the universe of items is not bounded, there is no way of actually measuring the true score. This means that we must use the statistical assumptions of the model discussed above to derive various features of it. The most important of these derivations are set out below.

1 The correlation with an item with the true score equals the square root of its average correlation with all other items. Since this last is observable, this means the correlation of an item with the true score can be estimated. It also means that if a test consists of items which intercorrelate highly, then each item (and hence the test score) must correlate highly with the true score. This is the theoretical basis of the insistence on high internal consistency reliability.

2 If we substitute tests for items in the above equation, all the

arguments hold for tests: hence, again, the importance of having parallel forms of tests which correlate highly with each other. In this application of the equation the tests are held to be random samples of items, and the test means and variances vary from each other due only to random error.

3   Reliability increases with the number of items and as the item intercorrelations rise.

4   The rate of increase of test reliability with increasing numbers of items can be calculated. Nunnally (1978) shows that with thirty items a very high reliability can be attained. Even fifteen items can yield highly reliable tests.

5   Coefficient alpha, which we have presented as the most important coefficient of reliability, can be derived from the model. It is the estimated correlation of the test with another test of the same length and composed of items from the same universe of items. Its square root is the estimated correlation of the test with the true score. Thus if coefficient alpha is low, according to the classical model, then the test cannot be satisfactory.

6   Finally – and this point is of great practical importance and yet another reason why high reliability is stressed so emphatically in psychometry – the standard error of measurement can be derived from the model. The standard error of measurement is the expected standard deviation of scores for a subject taking a number of subsets of items from the item universe (i.e. parallel forms of a test). In fact, the formula for the standard error of measurement derived from the model is: $\text{SEM} = \sigma x \mathbin{/} \sqrt{1 - r_{xx}}$, where σx is the standard deviation of the test and r_{xx} is its reliability.

In practice, we can say that, given the score of a subject, 68 per cent of his scores on the test would fall between plus and minus one standard error of measurement of the score, and 95 per cent would fall between plus and minus two standard errors. This means that if we want to use a personality test with an individual to form the basis of counselling or psychotherapy, we can be confident of the score only if the SEM is low and this is only low if the reliability is high. Guilford (1956) argues that where the reliability falls below 0.7, tests should not be used as a basis for decision-making.

Conclusions concerning the classical model of error measurement

We have included a brief description of this model so that readers may be aware that the psychometric bases on which tests are constructed have themselves a sound statistical rationale. This is important, since much of what we are to argue in later sections of this book depends on the results of personality testing.

Nevertheless, a few words of caution are necessary. As we have seen from the model, error and reliability are closely entwined. However, it does not follow from the model that reliable tests must be valid. That is a logical error. Unreliable tests must be compounded with error and yield scores different from the true scores. Reliable tests will yield scores approximating true scores. However, as it is statistical, the model does not specify the nature of the true score. Thus, if the true score (i.e. the score on the universe of items) is different from what we wish to measure, a perfectly reliable test will still be invalid. In other words, if the items do not reflect what we wish to measure, the test, however reliable, will not be valid.

Thus this model does not contradict our earlier claims that reliability is not a guarantee of validity. But does it contradict Cattell's claims that his tests, although unreliable, are still valid? In fact it does not; in terms of the model, Cattell would argue that his tests are measuring two highly correlated universes of items or, alternatively, that his universe of items is broader than that normally utilized by test constructors.

In sum, then, the model is useful in providing a basis for most psychometric indices of test efficiency, and in general it supports the psychometric demands for highly reliable tests.

Response sets

Before leaving the topic of validity and its statistical logical rationale, mention should be made of response sets. As the name suggests, these describe ways of responding to items independently of item content. Attention was first drawn to them by Cronbach (1946, 1950), and a huge research effort has been concentrated on them, notably by Edwards (1957). Their importance lies in the fact that they interfere with the validity of tests because they influence responses, sometimes to a greater extent than the item content. We shall simply describe the two most pervasive response sets.

Social desirability

This describes the tendency of subjects to endorse an item according to how socially desirable a response is. Edwards (1957), in his studies of social desirability, found that there was a significant correlation between the endorsement rate for personality test items and how socially desirable they were judged to be. Such findings, of course, cast doubt on the validity of all personality questionnaires, since subjects may not be responding to the items *per se* but merely to their perceived social desirability. This is why, *inter alia*, personality tests cannot be judged adequate or inadequate from a perusal of their items – why, indeed, their face validity is misleading. It is also a major reason why it is necessary to have sound evidence that a personality test is valid, because if it is, the question of social desirability becomes otiose.

Generally, if in test construction item writers are careful to avoid obviously socially desirable items and to eliminate items which have extremely unequal response splits, the worst effects of social desirability can be avoided. The solution used by Edwards (1970) in his own test, the Edwards Personal Preference Schedule (EPPS), was ingenious. He used forced/choice items; the members of each pair from which the choice was to be made were judged equal in social desirability. However, in our view such elaborate precautions are not necessary unless all validity studies fail.

In brief, social desirability is an important source of error in personality questionnaires, but it may be ignored if the tests are shown to be valid.

Acquiescence

This is a further source of error in personality questionnaires. Acquiescence is the tendency to agree with or to respond 'Yes' to an item, regardless of content. To avoid contaminating high scores on questionnaires with acquiescence, scales are constructed with equal numbers of items keyed 'Yes' and 'No' – for example, items tapping sarcasm: 'Are you known for your bitter tongue?' (this item is keyed 'Yes'); 'Do people think of you as mild and polite?' (this item is keyed 'No'). Such balanced scales do not really overcome the problem of acquiescence, but they do mean that high scorers are not simply acquiescent subjects.

Guilford (1959) has argued from his extensive experience of personality test construction that acquiescence may be minimized by writing items that are as specific as possible and refer to behaviours rather than feelings. After all, it is more difficult to reply 'Yes' to the item 'Do you play bowls?' if you do not than to the more general item 'Do you enjoy most sports?'

As with social desirability, the influence of acquiescence can be ignored if the test has a clearly demonstrated validity. However, there is no doubt that acquiescence can render personality tests of dubious value. The outstanding example of this is the F scale (Adorno *et al.*, 1950), which appears to measure Fascist tendencies. Numerous studies, summarized in Brown (1965), for example, have shown the scale to be hopelessly confounded with acquiescence. A balanced F scale produces quite different results.

In summary, users of personality tests must be aware of the dangers of response sets, but by insisting on high validity they may be assured that the tests are not ruined by these unwanted variables.

Finally, we shall deal with two other important general issues in psychological tests: norms and standardization, and a relatively recent innovation which, if found successful, would make normalization unnecessary – Rasch scaling (Rasch, 1966).

Norms and standardization

One advantage of personality inventories over other forms of personality assessment is that with such tests it is easier to establish good norms. Norms are simply sets of scores on the particular test against which it is possible meaningfully to interpret any given score – either of an individual or a group mean. For example, a score of X on test Y is not interpretable out of context. However, if it is known from the norms that only depressives score X or higher, then such a score becomes pregnant with possibilities.

Two important points should be made about norms.

1 Norms are useful only if the population on which they have been established has been properly sampled. Some personality tests have norms based on groups, such as fifteen airline hostesses and twenty-three electrical contractors, with no details of sampling procedures. Such small groups almost inevitably fail to constitute a proper sample, however the sampling procedures are carried out.

2 Although percentiles (the score below which a given proportion of the population falls) are easily comprehensible, they suffer from the disadvantage that they are unsuited to statistical analysis. More useful are norms, such as T scores, which have fixed means and

standard deviations and are normally distributed. If normal distributions are not built into the norms themselves, then some indication of the distribution of scores should be given.

Properly sampled and calibrated norms indubitably add meaning to test scores, and they are a useful adjunct to any personality test.

The Rasch simple logistic response model

Rasch scaling (Rasch, 1960) is an approach to testing that has many advantages, it has been claimed, by comparison with the classical psychometric approach. Our treatment will not be detailed, partly because the necessary mathematics are so formidable and partly because there are disputes among the experts (e.g. Levy, 1973) as to its value. In addition, it has been little used in practice, so that its efficacy, as distinct from its mathematical limitations, is hard to assess.

The point of this model is (a) to allow computation of the internal consistency of a scale, irrespective of the variance in the population being tested and (b) to identify any item–population interactions which render dubious the comparison of populations. In practice, this means that Rasch analysis yields item difficulties that are independent of the subjects from whom the test scores forming the basis of the calculations are derived and trait scores independent of the items actually taken. Thus Rasch analysis allows subsets of items to be used, each subset yielding the same score. In addition, there is a true zero. So if all these claims were indisputable, Rasch analysis would provide ideal tests, since these would be applicable to any group and would be ratio scales.

Basic assumptions of the Rasch model

The Rasch model assumes that the probability of a subject's response to an item is a function of his status on the variable and the facility the item has in eliciting this status. The higher a subject's status and the facility level of the item, the greater the probability that he will respond according to the score key.

The procedures of Rasch scaling, which we shall not describe here, are aimed at estimating subjects' trait levels independently of the item difficulties, and item difficulties independently of the trait levels, often by maximum-likelihood procedures. In addition, statistical tests are made to see whether or not items fit the model. Rasch (1961) contains details of the complex computational procedures.

From the viewpoint of personality testing, the value of Rasch scaling lies in its capacity to produce population-free item statistics which should admit of cross-cultural testing. In addition, the ability to utilize equivalent subsets of items is useful for longitudinal and developmental studies. What must now be examined, therefore, is the extent to which these claims for Rasch scaling can stand critical evaluation.

Evaluation of the Rasch model

First, as Levy (1973) points out, it must be appreciated that the Rasch model is only one of a set of models based upon item characteristics, models which are fully described in Lord and Novick (1968). Some of the objections to, and problems with, the model are overcome to some extent by yet more complex variants. However, these have not been used in practical test construction and are of theoretical interest only to specialists in item characteristic curves. These objections are more fully described in Nunnally (1978), whose succinct arguments are most helpful.

Some of the more detailed assumptions of the Rasch model are almost certainly wrong: that items are equally discriminating, that no guessing takes place, that only one trait runs through the items. Certainly, an extra parameter to cope with guessing can be inserted into the Rasch model, but if this is done, the procedures become too unwieldy for practical test application.

Furthermore, as Lord (1974) points out, huge samples have to be tested if reliable, population-free calibration is to be successful. In addition, experience with attainment testing (e.g. Chopin, 1976) indicates that often items do not fit the model, and in any case there is considerable disagreement over appropriate statistical procedures to measure item fit. To make matters worse, Wood (1978) showed that random data, coin tossing, could be made to fit the Rasch model. Finally, Nunnally argues that in any case there is a very high correlation between Rasch scales and scales made to fit the classical model.

For all these reasons we decided not to spend more time on expounding the Rasch model. However, we have included it because, in our view, despite these problems, empirical studies are worthwhile. For it may be that the Rasch model will yield valid and population-free scales even if some of the assumptions are violated, and if this is the case, it will turn out to be a useful method. Certainly, Andrich and Kline (1981) working with a personality test in two very different cultures, found the method of some value. Experimental studies of Rasch-scaled personality tests are urgently needed.

Summary

Some general problems of measurement with respect, especially, to personality testing have been discussed:

1   Types of scale
2   Reliability of tests
3   Validity of tests
4   Discriminatory power of tests
5   The classical model of measurement error
6   Response sets
7   Norms and standardization
8   Rasch scaling

2 Different methods of personality assessment

With the demands of good testing (discussed in the first chapter) in mind, we are now almost ready to examine the various methods of personality assessment that have been tried over the years. This chapter, therefore, will consist of a discussion of interviews, behavioural observations, rating scales, repertory grids, semantic differentials and psychological personality tests, against the backcloth of reliability and validity.

However, before this scrutiny can begin it is essential to define what is meant by personality. Over the years, as Hall and Lindzey (1957) point out, a huge variety of definitions has arisen, many dependent upon the particular orientation of their authors. The view taken here is similarly adapted to our approach, which, of course, is psychometric. Indeed, the meaning of personality is implied in the psychometric model of man which has been essentially described elsewhere (Kline, 1980d).

In the psychometric model of man it is assumed that any given behaviour is a linear function of ability traits, temperamental traits, motivational traits, moods and the situation in which an individual finds himself. This model, with its profound implications for the study of personality and views of traits and situations, is fully examined in Chapter 8. The definition of personality implicit in the model is that it is the sum total of the characteristics (traits) of an individual which contribute to his behaviour, to his being himself, different from others. However, because ability traits tend to form a distinct cluster of traits, distinct from the others, these are not generally included in the definition of personality, which is conceived of as comprising temperamental and dynamic traits. It is a definition of personality based upon individual differences.

With this view of personality, therefore, the aim of personality assessment is to elucidate these traits. In fact, as we have argued, because traits of ability are not included in the definition, personality assessment is not concerned with the measurement of abilities.

In the light of this definition and in the context of the demands of good measurement, we shall evaluate the different methods of personality assessment to be found in psychological research. We shall begin with the simplest, least technical procedure and the one most widely used – the interview.

The interview

Of all assessment procedures, interviews are probably the most common. However, we intend to say little about them, since there is a good consensus of agreement that they are highly ineffective, especially in respect of personality measurement. Vernon and Parry (1949), who used interviews in War Office selection methods and examined their efficiency, were forced to conclude that interviews should be used only to obtain information for which no tests exist. This is not to deny that there are some individuals who are particularly good at interviewing, but these are too few to be useful as assessors and are only recognizable *post hoc*. Furthermore, there is little evidence that such individuals would be good at measuring the traits necessary for the study of personality as defined in the psychometric model. Vernon (1964), writing on personality assessment, argued that interviews used as selection devices added only noise. Nor has more recent work done anything to change these judgements radically.

Generally, in the terms that we have discussed measurement, interviews fail because they are not reliable. There are considerable differences between interviewers and, if the same subjects are interviewed more than once, between occasions. Similarly, studies of the validity of interviews are equally disappointing. Thus in terms of reliability and validity, interviews are poor. Again, from the nature of the interview we could not expect to obtain a highly discriminating measure, since nine categories are about the maximum that an individual can hold in his mind. All these points are discussed fully in Vernon and Parry (1949) and Vernon (1964). Psychometrically, therefore, interviews are exceedingly weak.

Since the aim of interviews, from the viewpoint of personality measurement, is to measure traits, again one is forced to conclude that the interview is particularly unsuitable. Vernon and Parry and Shouksmith (1968), in trying to find some place for the interview, agree that it is at its best where the actual behaviour that one is attempting to measure can be observed during the interview (for example, ability at intricate argument or verbal fluency). Conversely, it is at its worst where inferences have to be made, and this is precisely what has to be done if the interview is to be used as a means of personality-trait assessment.

To sum up: the interview is not recommended as a means of personality assessment, and data obtained by this method are not regarded by this author as scientifically useful.

Nevertheless, almost all researchers in the field of personality research (see especially Shouksmith, 1968; Vernon and Parry, 1949), agree that personal information can be extracted from interviews more easily (and with greater accuracy) than by most other techniques and that this is their strong point if interviews are properly conducted. One possible use of the interview in personality research, therefore, is to design interviews to obtain certain specific personal data and to analyse these statistically, together with personality and motivation test scores. In this way interview data could throw important light on the environmental events important in the development of certain personality factors. The quantitative analysis of personality tests traits, combined with interview data, could be important in the study of personality, but this is the only use of the interview that we regard as viable, and it is a far cry from the interview used as a method of personality assessment.

Rating scales

Another approach to the measurement of personality is the rating scale. For example, subjects can be rated on five- or seven-point scales for such characteristics as bravery, toughness or generosity. The rater would have to indicate whether a subject always/often/some-times/occasionally/never displayed these traits. However, there are severe problems with ratings used for personality assessment, which have been succinctly summarized by Cattell and Kline (1977):

1 To rate properly, raters have to observe their subjects not only for long periods but in a wide variety of situations.
2 Being observed affects behaviour. These effects can be overcome only when the raters have been at work so often that they are simply, from the subject's point of view, part of the background.
3 The 'halo effect' can distort ratings: subjects rated high for one variable tend to be rated high for others.
4 Inter-rater reliability and the reliability of the ratings of raters on different occasions is not usually high.

5   Ratings to some extent reflect the response style of the rater, in that some raters avoid extremes, while others favour them.

These difficulties obviously render the validity of ratings dubious. Since the first point, the necessity for observations of a wide variety of behaviours, demands time sampling, there are obvious practical difficulties in assessing personality by this method.

However, it is to be noted that Cattell (e.g. 1946, 1957), who is one of the leading figures in this field, used ratings as the basis for his forty years' research into the main personality traits, although recently Howarth (1976) has called the findings into question (but *not* on the basis of the rating methods).

Cattell (e.g. 1957) claims that ratings can be used for the assessment of personality traits if the following points are observed.

1   Subjects should be observed in a wide variety of circumstances and on many occasions, for reasons that we have mentioned above. This Cattell calls 'implicit time sampling'. This, of course, is an excellent idea but one that makes the practice of such rating extremely difficult.
2   Observations should continue for a year if possible, and certainly not less than three months, in order to ensure the implicit time sampling of point one. Such a procedure shows up the obvious weakness of the interview.
3   The traits should be defined in terms of behaviours at the various points of the scale. This does much to eliminate rater differences. For example, the behaviours that would cause raters to rate subjects as 'extremely cheerful' would be set out thus: 'Laughs at every opportunity', 'Does not complain even when all goes wrong' and so on.
4   To eliminate rater differences in using the scale, subjects should be ranked using paired comparisons, and the ranks should be converted to standard scores.
5   Peer ratings should be used where possible, since the roles of raters and their relationship to subjects can affect their behaviour: interviewers, teachers, counsellors, judges – all these role relationships would surely distort behaviour.
6   There should be more than ten raters for each subject. This increases both the reliability and the validity of ratings, since each judge will add some component of the common-factor variance. Of course, if judges do not know the subject well, they will add error

variance; hence there must be a limit on the number of judges.
7 The 'halo effect' can be reduced by having subjects rated for only one trait at a time. In addition, point 3 must considerably reduce 'halo effects'.
8 Judges should have their mean ratings made equal. Since in such a complex rating system it is bound to be the case that not all subjects will be rated by judges for all traits, a small common calibration sample would have to be used.
9 Judges should rate independently.

It seems to us that this rating scheme does, in fact, overcome most of the objections to rating as a means of personality assessment. Providing that behaviours defining traits can be specified, there is no reason why valid and reliable results should not be obtained. Such ratings could then be analysed by multivariate methods and the main factors extracted.

Certainly, the claims of Mischel (1968) that raters who rate subjects they have seen for about a minute produce ratings with a structure little different from that of Cattell's raters using these methods, and that therefore such ratings reflect not the subjects' behaviour but the raters' categorizing of behaviour, cannot hold up. All that Mischel's work indicates is that if forced by the somewhat absurd experimental demand to make immediate judgements about personality, conventional character stereotypes do resemble genuine observations. The resemblance can in no way impugn observations properly made according to the Cattellian system.

The real objection to the rating system proposed by Cattell is its impracticality. Not only would it be extremely difficult to arrange for such a system to run for a year in any institution, but the costs would be prohibitive given the probable outcome. In addition, and this is another severe objection, the samples that can be rated in this way would almost inevitably have to come from institutions. Random sampling would be impossible. This coupled with the fact that samples would have to be limited in size, contraindicates the method. Certainly, Cattell and his colleagues who have indisputably carried out the most intensive research into the psychometry of personality were forced to abandon the method. However, it is to be noted that their other assessment methods were always compared with ratings, i.e. ratings were the criterion-targets of their other kinds of assessment.

In summary, ratings are usually unreliable and of low validity. Methods necessary to improve them can be devised, but are so cumbrous that they make data collection on any scale almost impossible.

Behavioural observations

Mention here should be made of behavioural observations, a technique frequently used by behaviour modifiers (see Samson, 1972, for a full description). In this, frequency counts of the behaviours of which it is desired to increase or decrease the occurrence are made before and after conditioning. This allows for statistical analysis and comparison with untreated groups and groups treated by other, putatively inferior, psychotherapies. However, the problems in this method are precisely those of the rating methods mentioned above. If, however, the observed behaviours are clear-cut, e.g. number of eye contacts per unit of time, or number of obscenities uttered per unit of time, the kind of variable in this type of research, the method is viable especially with in-patient groups. For the more pervasive behavioural measurement in samples of all kinds required by the psychometric approach, the method is not suitable for the reasons applicable to Cattell's rating methods.

Semantic differentials

We shall deal briefly with these possible methods of assessing personality, although, as we shall see, neither is pertinent to our purposes. The semantic differential which was developed by Osgood *et al.* (1957) is effectively a set of seven-point bipolar rating scales. Osgood *et al.* claimed that analysis of the ratings revealed that three factors could account for much of the variance underlying ratings – factors of potency, activity and evaluation.

In the semantic-rating scale technique subjects are required to rate given elements, e.g. myself, and myself as I would like to be, on constructs, e.g. bold/cowardly, clever/dull. From the viewpoint of personality, however, the relevance of the technique is that it is possible to compare scores of different groups on variables such as self-esteem, measured by the discrepancy between self and ideal self, in relation to the effect of psychotherapy, or school refusal, to take two obvious examples.

The problem with the semantic differential is that the validity of the bipolar scales in most studies is only face validity. There is virtually no clear evidence that any given set of scales effectively measures a personality variable. Semantic differential results are usually used as if the ratings accurately reflect the subjects' feelings and attitudes, much as clinical psychologists use clinical evidence. This, of course, is not satisfactory as a basis for measurements. If, in addition, the scales are really loaded on three factors of potency evaluation and goodness, there is even less reason to so interpret them.

Furthermore there is a characteristic of the semantic differential which for this writer makes its use highly dubious (until powerful evidence of validity is presented). In many cases subjects are required to rate elements for constructs which are quite foreign to them and may appear absurd. These demand characteristics (Orne, 1962) may mean that results from the semantic differential are not generalizable beyond that frame of reference, that all factors are specific semantic differential factors.

In brief until a set of semantic differential scales is produced with good evidence for validity, it would seem hazardous to rely on them as a basis for the measurement of personality.

Repertory grids

A repertory grid, like the semantic differential, consists essentially of elements and constructs. The elements have to be ranked in respect of the constructs or rated. They can consist of anything in the subject's life, although usually they are the persons or things most important to him, just as the constructs are usually those most pertinent to the subject. However, unlike the semantic differential – and this is what makes the repertory grid so distinctive, as Bannister and Mair (1968) argue – *the elements and constructs* are elicited from the subjects. Thus strictly no one subject can be compared with any other, and in this sense the repertory grid is not a test at all. Each person is evaluated within his own terms.

The theoretical approach within which the repertory grid was developed is that of Kelly (1955), who claimed that a person cannot be understood until we know how he construes the world – hence the term construct theory. According to this view, man is the scientist who hypothesizes all the time to account for what is happening to him and around him. These hypotheses are framed uniquely for each individual, and the grid is the basic method advocated by Kelly to understand an individual's constructs.

Its main use at present, in Britain at least, is in clinical psychology and psychotherapy. Thus the Kellian view of a subject's, say, marital problems would be that his view of marriage, the way he construes it, is very different from that of his partner. In any case such marital problems could not be understood by the psychotherapist unless he knew that subject's views. These, then, can be ascertained from the repertory grid.

There is now considerable sophistication in the construction and analysis of grids (e.g. Slater, 1964). What we shall describe here is the basic form (of which others are but elaborations) as this most clearly indicates the nature of the grid and shows that it is essentially not useful for our purposes as a basis of measurement in personality.

For our description of the grid we shall take our marital example. The basic aim of the grid is to explicate our subject's view of marriage and his spouse. The grid in this instance will consist of elements that we consider to be important in this case: spouse, sex, money, housework, arguments, parents, parents-in-law, children, for example. As we have mentioned, the distinctive feature of the repertory grid lies in the fact that the constructs are the client's own, not some arbitrary set considered important by the psychologist. Hence the client's own constructs concerning these elements are obtained. One method is to get our subject to discriminate between any triad of the set. For example, he might say: My parents were kind but my wife is vicious. This gives us our first construct *kind/vicious*. Again, we might obtain: children and money are pleasure giving, but sex is painful. In this way the constructs with which the subject perceives his marriage may be obtained. When ten or so constructs have been elicited, subjects rank or rate the elements on these constructs.

As we have mentioned, the statistical analyses of grids are highly complex, and we shall not go into details here. However, the aim of the analysis is two-fold: to find which elements are construed as similar and how they are construed, and which constructs are also related. Thus we might find that the patient thought of sex as painful and boring and had a view of it as closely related to arguments. Similarly it might emerge that his spouse was equated with the spouse's mother. As regards construct similarity, this can be useful and revealing. Thus, if a subject construes similarity, this can be useful and revealing. Thus, if a subject construes together cruel and intelligent and his spouse is intelligent, then somehow that equation demands changing.

This brief description (fully amplified in Bannister and Mair, 1968) illustrates clearly the points we wish to make about repertory grids. In the first place, because grids use elicited constructs there is no way of comparing acts to results. Even if by chance two subjects used the same set of construct terms, their interrelationships and thus their meaning and significance for the individual would be almost certainly different; hence comparison here, in the context of grid theory would not be sensible. The uniqueness of each grid means that for the trait approach, the psychometric model, conceived of in terms of individual differences the grid is inherently unsuited.

The second point is that in essence the grid is a formalized, roughly quantified interview. All the information is elicited in a straightforward way from the subject. As such, it is probably highly useful for clinical psychology, but twenty years of intensive repertory grid work has failed to yield much scientific information, as even Fransella (1980) a keen practitioner, admits. In summary the repertory grid is not suited to the task of eliciting the main personality traits, necessary for elucidating the psychometric model of man.

Psychological tests

We now come to what, for our purposes, are indubitably the most powerful form of psychological assessment in the field of personality – psychological tests. There are generally considered to be three kinds of personality test: personality questionnaires, projective tests and objective tests defined by Cattell (e.g. Cattell and Kline, 1977) as tests which can be objectively scored and of which the true purpose is hidden from the subjects. However, as we shall see, projective tests, the oldest approach in this field, can be included in the category of objective tests, if specially scored. We shall retain the projective test category, nevertheless, because it is one hallowed by tradition and usage and it would seem wrong to rename the most famous examples, e.g. the Rorschach and the TAT. In addition there are a few tests which fall outside these categories and these will be mentioned where most appropriate.

In this chapter, which is an overview of the different types of personality assessment, we shall not go into details of test construction or compare different varieties because this will be done in succeeding chapters of this book. Here we shall compare their relative qualities in the light of the demands of good tests and the needs of the psychometric approach to personality.

Personality questionnaires

Personality questionnaires consist of (in the main) sets of items concerned with behaviour. Subjects have to indicate whether they respond as the item suggests. Items are often of the yes/no or true/false variety. Other item formats are possible and these will be discussed in subsequent chapters.

Typical items   'Do you have vivid dreams?' 'Are you easily upset by criticism?' 'Are you regarded as quiet and retiring?'

Reliability   Questionnaires can be made highly reliable, although there is usually more item variation than in tests of intellectual ability. There is no reason to use questionnaires with reliabilities lower than 5, and some may have reliabilities well beyond this figure. Clearly, there is no inter-marker unreliability to add confusion.

Validity   For personality questionnaires construct validity is the most convincing evidence to be adduced. The best tests of the largest personality factors, extraversion and neuroticism, have convincing construct validity. Many tests, however, as references to Buros's *Mental Measurement Yearbooks* (e.g. Buros, 1978) indicate, have little more than face validity, so their results have to be treated with considerable caution.

Discriminatory power   Although discriminatory power is rarely quoted, most questionnaires by virtue of length and consequent variance are reasonably discriminating, far more so than any of the assessment methods so far discussed. Thus, from the viewpoint of psychometric efficiency, personality questionnaires *can* be good.

Personality questionnaires fall broadly into two groups, differing in method of construction. One group includes tests where the items are selected for a particular scale if they can discriminate one criterion group from controls. These tests are often highly valuable in applied psychology, but from the viewpoint of measuring the most important personality traits are not necessarily useful. This is because any criterion group may differ on a variety of variables from controls, and the mere fact of discrimination tells us nothing about the variables contributing to such discrimination.

The second group, in principle, are more valuable for the scientific study of personality. Indeed many of the tests were devised precisely to discover the most important personality traits. These tests are constructed by factor-analysing the intercorrelations between person-ality test items, and items are selected if they load clearly on one factor. There are many problems with such factored questionnaires despite their theoretical at-ractiveness, and these, together with difficulties of the first category of personality tests, will be fully discussed in Chapter 3.

At this juncture, however, it is sufficient to note that factored personality tests, if well constructed, are highly suited to the psychometric study of personality. Many of the findings to be discussed throughout this book have been derived from tests thus constructed.

In summary, the factored personality questionnaire is a powerful measuring device for the study of personality, given that its problems and difficulties can be overcome.

Projective tests

Projective tests usually consist of ambiguous stimuli to which subjects are required to respond, often by description. The first (and most famous) personality test was of this kind: the Rorschach test (Rorschach, 1921), consisting of ten symmetrical ink blots, being the archetypal projective measure and to many outside the field the archetypal psychological test.

Whereas personality questionnaires have been deliberately designed to measure the traits and dimensions common to all, on which people vary, variations which are considered to be the essence of personality, projective tests are held by their adherents to do virtually the opposite of this. They are held to measure the idiodynamics of a subject (Rosenzweig, 1951), i.e. the innermost thoughts and feelings of an individual, all those aspects of a person which are particular to him and him alone, the essence, that is, of his individuality. The term 'projective' is used because, since the stimulus is vague, often so vague that a veridical description is impossible, it is argued that the description which, in fact, most subjects give must arise from the subject himself; thus he has projected something of himself on to the stimulus. Clearly, on this rationale, if the stimulus were clear, the description would be almost entirely stimulus-bound.

Eysenck (1959) launched a fierce attack on the Rorschach test in particular and projective tests in general on the grounds that there was little evidence for their validity and that they were mere vehicles for the riotous imaginations of clinicians. Certainly, the need to interpret projective test responses, in the standard interpretative procedures, leads inevitably to poor reliability, both between scorers and on different occasions. Certainly too, Vernon (1964) has assembled sufficient evidence to show that projective test responses are affected by external variables such as the sex or race of the examiner, the examiner's mood and the view the subject has of the test. Thus, it is doubtful whether they can be measuring any aspect of the deeper personality, as is claimed. It is also generally true that most validity studies are inadequate in respect of research design.

Since, in addition, the approach of projective tests is opposed to the one adopted in the psychometric-trait view, it might appear that projective tests would be useless for our purposes.

However, when we come to describe projective tests in Chapter 5, we shall devote ourselves to an examination of some attempts to overcome many of the defects which we have discussed, attempts which already in some cases have yielded impressive results. In summary, we argue that the projective test as traditionally used is far too unreliable and invalid to be valuable in scientific research. However, new methods of scoring and analysis may reveal their full potential.

Objective tests

Objective personality tests – defined, again, as tests which can be objectively scored and whose true purpose is hidden from subjects, thus avoiding wilful distortion – have been developed by Eysenck and his colleagues at the Maudsley Hospital and by Cattell and his research group at Illinois. These last have published extensively on the subject, especially useful being the *Compendium of Objective Tests* (Cattell and Warburton, 1965). In this compendium more than 800 objective tests are described, from which about 2000 variables can be derived.

In principle, objective tests are probably the best of all the assessment techniques that we have discussed. Their resistance to wilful distortion means that they can be used in selection and guidance with some confidence, and their lack of reliance on personal insights also means that less obvious distortions such as social desirability, are rendered trivial. In practice, however, the vast majority of objective tests have little evidence for validity, so that they can be used only in research and then with the utmost caution. Few sets of objective tests have been published and those that have, e.g. the Objective Analytic Test Battery (Cattell and Schuerger, 1978) are certainly not well supported by evidence of validity. In addition many of the tests require laboratories for their administration so that unless there is powerful evidence in their favour, psychologists are not usually willing to try them. This lack of validity, indeed, is due largely to practical problems and the reluctance to use strange new tests, rather than to demonstrated invalidity.

This brief description of objective personality tests, instruments of infinite promise, ends with a few examples.

1 *The fidgetometer* A special chair records all movements made by the subject.
2 *The balloon test* Subjects inflate a balloon. Variables are the size of the balloon, time taken blowing it up, whether it is burst or not.
3 *The slow line-drawing test* Subjects are required to draw a line as slowly as possible for a given time.

So much for objective tests, the source of Cattell's T data. As can be seen from the description, projective tests, if objectively scored, would fall into this category. In summary, objective tests are potentially useful but require considerable research before they can be confidently used.

Summary

The different methods of personality assessment have been scrutinized in the context of the psychometric demands of good tests and the psychometric-trait view of man.

1 Interviews
2 Rating scales
3 Behavioural observations
4 Semantic differentials
5 Repertory grids
6 Psychological tests
   (a) Inventories
   (b) Projective tests
   (c) Objective tests

Of all these methods, psychological tests were shown to be the most suitable basis for the scientific study of personality.

3 Psychological tests of personality 1: personality questionnaires

In the previous chapter we briefly described personality questionnaires or inventories as consisting of lists of statements or questions about behaviour. In our more detailed scrutiny of these tests we shall attempt to answer the obvious questions of what form the items take, how the items come to be written, how they are selected for particular scales: in fact, the whole rationale of the construction of such tests will be revealed. In addition, we shall describe the best-known personality questionnaires.

Item formats

The kinds of item typical of most personality tests are set out below.

The yes/no item

Simple to write and easy to answer, this is the form of item favoured by Eysenck for his various personality questionnaires – the MPI (Eysenck, 1956), the EPI (Eysenck and Eysenck, 1964) and the EPQ (Eysenck and Eysenck, 1975). A typical item is 'Do you enjoy rare steaks?' A variant of this item type has a middle, uncertain category because subjects object to being forced to respond yes or no to items about which they feel almost nothing.

Bendig (1959) found in comparing dichotomous and trichotomous forms of the MPI that there was a high correlation between the two, and he concluded that probably the former was the better because it forced choice and that the uncertain category is not informative. Cattell and colleagues, in their well-known personality tests, use this trichotomous form for some of their items.

The true/false item

This is the item form used in the MMPI (Hathaway and McKinley, 1951). The statements are usually couched in the first person, and subjects are required to indicate whether they are true or false for them. Clearly, these items are very similar to those above. A typical item is 'My mother always hated me.'

The single word or phrase (to which subjects respond like/dislike)

An item form of great ingenuity (the art that hides art) and attractiveness for subjects. This form, used by Grygier (1961) in the Dynamic Personality Inventory, is found in its forerunner, the Krout Personal Preference Scale (Krout and Tabin, 1954), and by Wilson and Patterson in the Conservatism Scale (Wilson and Patterson, 1970).

Obviously, in constructing such items the skill lies in knowing the words to choose. This is a good item form, tending by its simplicity to minimize acquiescence, and is one rather easy to write with low social desirability. Typical items might be marine monsters, the sound of the saxophone, bantams.

Items with rating scales

Comrey (1970) uses these items in his test. Subjects respond on scales always/never or definitely/definitely not. Although subjects prefer such scaled responses to dichotomous items, there are obviously difficulties over the interpretation of the frequency terms of the scale. Such seven- or nine-point scales have statistical advantages over dichotomous items when item intercorrelations are required. A typical item might be 'I am assertive in crowds: always ... never.'

Trichotomous variants of yes/no and true/false items

These allow for more flexible item writing. Typical formats are generally, sometimes, never, true, uncertain, false, agree, uncertain, disagree, often, occasionally, never.

Forced-choice items

These are used by Edwards (1957), in his Personal Preference Schedule constructed to overcome the influence of social desirability, and by Briggs and Myers (1962) in their well-known Jungian test. In this format two or more statements are set out, and subjects have to choose one. A typical item might read thus: 'If I want a book to read, I prefer (a) a classic novel, (b) a biography, (c) a romance.'

These are the main item types, and most inventories of any repute utilize them. However, one other well-known test, the Adjective Check List (Gough, 1965), consists of adjectives, and subjects indicate whether each one is descriptive of them.

So much for the forms of items. We must now consider the probably more critical problem of item writing. How are personality-test items chosen for trial in scales?

The provenance of items

In the 1920s Woodworth developed one of the first questionnaire measures of anxiety by going through the psychiatric descriptions of the state and putting them into item form. Essentially, this is the method still in use today. For example, the present author has recently constructed two personality inventories, OPQ and OOQ, measuring, it is claimed, the oral, pessimistic and optimistic characters (Kline, 1980a). For this the psychoanalytic descriptions of the oral character were searched (e.g. Abraham, 1921; Glover, 1924), and all descriptive trait terms were extracted, together with any examples of actual behaviour. This list of traits and behaviours was then converted, with as little change as possible (given the author's skill at item writing, which may, of course, be limited), to items of the yes/no variety. Care was taken to avoid social desirability, and acquiescence was taken into account by writing items with oral responses keyed no.

A few examples will illustrate the points. Let it be said that these tests are being used as illustrations not because they are considered particularly excellent but because, obviously, the precise provenance of the items is known.

1 Optimism: 'Is the environment going to be destroyed by pollution in the next fifty years?'
2 Easy-going cheerfulness: 'Life's good when you just relax.'
3 Liking children: 'Are you good with children?'

It must be stressed at this juncture that items are not selected for scales on the basis of their resemblance to the relevant psychological description. Selection is based on the empirical demonstration that items do measure what is intended, and it is to this aspect of personality-test construction that we must now turn, for a proper understanding of the methods of personality-test construction, given that these procedures have been efficiently executed, shows that many objections to personality inventories are fatuous and that valuable psychological information can be extracted from them.

In this section we shall not go into the details of test construction for their own sake. Rather, we shall be concerned with the principles, although sufficient detail will be given, where this is necessary, to elucidate the problems and difficulties which, unless they are correctly dealt with, can render the methods dubious. For a full description of the practice of test construction, readers should turn to Nunnally (1978) or Kline (1982).

There are two basic approaches to the construction of personality inventories, which are fundamentally different. These will be described and scrutinized separately. These methods are concerned with the selection of items from an item pool.

The criterion-keyed method

In this approach items are selected if they can discriminate a criterion group or groups from controls. The best-known personality inventory constructed by this method is the Minnesota Multiphasic Personality Inventory, the MMPI (Hathaway and McKinley, 1951). This test, consisting of 559 items, has nine clinical scales assessing subjects' status in respect of the main Kraepelinian clinical categories, such as manic depression, schizophrenia and paranoia. Items are selected for a particular scale if they can discriminate patients of the relevant group from other patients and normal controls. The authors regarded their test as essentially an item pool which would be used with any abnormal group for developing scales, and in fact more than 200 scales have been thus developed (Dahlstrom and Welsh, 1960).

This is clearly a simple method in principle. Any group can be set up as the criterion, and if discriminatory items can be written, a scale can be constructed. Obviously, all items should be cross-validated (that is, given to another, similar group to obviate the effects of chance in item selection).

There are logical problems associated with this method which, in our view, render this approach to test construction less than ideal.

The difficulty of establishing criterion groups

This is especially true of clinical tests, such as the MMPI, in connection with which there is often dispute concerning clinical diagnosis. Thus even if the scales could discriminate the Minnesota groups, they will not necessarily be as successful with groups classified by other psychiatrists who have received different training. For certain variables the establishment of criterion groups is almost out of the question. In the construction of our oral tests, for example, this method could not be used.

The meaning of the scales

Unless it so happens that the criterion group discriminated by the test items differs on only one variable (and this is, *a priori*, generally unlikely), then any scale based on its ability to discriminate may measure more than one variable. The ability to discriminate a group, furthermore, gives us no definite indication of what the variables are. Consequently, scales developed by criterion keying are intrinsically psychologically meaningless. They are likely to measure a hotchpotch of variables on which the relevant groups happen to differ.

From this two evils follow. In the first place, use of the scales yields no psychological knowledge because the meaning of the scales is unclear. Second, even if the variables in the scale have been identified, scores that are composites of more than one variable are not identical in meaning. Thus if we have a two-variable scale, a score of 10 can obviously consist of $10 + 0, 9 + 1$ and so on. This is one reason why psychometrists prefer a unidimensional, unifactorial scale. Strictly, of course, a non-univariate scale is not drawn from one universe of items and hence many of the derivations of the classical model of measurement (see Chapter 10) do not fit.

For all these reasons, especially the problem of psychological meaning, this form of test construction, although yielding tests of practical value, does not seem as useful as the factor-analytic and item-analytic methods, now to be described.

The factor- and item-analytic methods

The aim of the factor-analytic and item-analytic methods is to produce a homogeneous scale clearly measuring one variable. This method-ology, therefore, conforms to the classical model of error measurement that we discussed in Chapter 1, the assumption being that the homogeneity of the scale reflects the fact that the items come from the same universe of items. Of course, once the univariate scale has been produced, it is necessary to demonstrate what this variable is – that is, its validity has to be demonstrated.

So that the problems of these methods can be properly understood and, more important, so that the real advantages of the method can be grasped, it is necessary to insert a brief note on factor analysis. We shall not go into the mathematical techniques, which are fully explained in Harman (1976) and Cattell (1978). Instead we shall explain their logic and describe some of the widely used techniques.

What is a factor?

A factor is a linear combination of variables. So if in an item set we took the scores on items 1, 2, and 3, these could be a factor in the item set. We could weight the items in this factor either equally (i.e. we could just add them up) or differentially. This linear combination of variables can be conceived of as a dimension or construct.

Factor loadings

Factor loadings are the correlations of the variables in the data with the factors. Thus if item 1 loads 0.6 on factor 1, item 2 loads 0.5 and item 3 loads 0.8, these loadings enable us to identify the factor or dimension, for a factor is defined by its factor loadings. Thus, to identify our example factor, we would look for a construct that correlates 0.6 with item 1, 0.5 with item 2 and 0.8 with item 3. The answer would, of course, depend on the item content. To take an easy example, a factor that loads highly on scores on Greek, Latin, speed at *The Times* crossword and high ranking in the Civil Service is probably verbal ability. Thus factor loadings enable us to define constructs operationally (by the scores on the tests loading on the factor).

The common use of factor analysis in psychology

Factor analysis is a technique mainly used to simplify correlation matrices. Instead of attempting to understand all the correlations between a large set of variables, which is literally beyond the capacity of the human brain, the correlation matrix is subjected to factor analysis. Factors (linear combinations of the variables) are calculated which by cross-multiplication of the factor loadings can reproduce the original correlations. Thus a large set of intercorrelations can be understood in terms of a few factors.

An example from the field of human abilities will clarify the point. Suppose we have measured a large variety of abilities in a large sample of adults and have correlated the scores. The question that factor analysis can answer is this: what is the simplest way of accounting for the observed correlations between the ability tests? Generally research in the field of human abilities shows that four factors can account for these correlations (see Cattell, 1971b; Kline, 1979):

1 g, a general factor of reasoning ability on which all tests load, albeit some more than others;
2 V, a factor of verbal ability on which all tests concerned with verbal skills load;
3 N, numerical ability;
4 K, spatial ability, on which tests involving the ability to orient and visualize spatial configurations load.

Thus if we know subjects' scores on these four factors, we can account for the observed correlations between the ability variables. Note that these factors are defined and identified through their factor loadings. Such identification can be validated by later experimental studies. In the case of item factoring in test construction, we are looking for items that load highly on one factor only. In this way we can argue that the item variance is accounted for by one factor (i.e. the test is homogeneous).

There are various techniques of factor analysis, each yielding somewhat different results, and we must now consider the general problem of the identification, interpretation and replicability of factors.

A major difficulty with factor analysis is the fact that there is an infinite number of possible solutions, all mathematically equivalent. This has led some critics of the technique (e.g. Heim, 1975) to argue that it is a virtually worthless technique. However, those who understand the method – Cattell, Eysenck and Guilford, to name the leading workers in the factor analysis of personality – have easily overcome this problem, and we must now also look at this essential aspect of the factor-analytic method.

Principal components analysis

Since many computer programmes for factor analysis begin with principal components analysis, we shall discuss the problem beginning from this point, although the arguments hold for all other techniques.

Principal components analysis provides us with the first set of factors accounting for the intercorrelations. By virtue of the computational algebra, principal components yield a general factor followed by bipolar factors (i.e. factors loaded negatively on some variables, positively on others). The factors are arranged in decreasing order of variance accounted for, and in this technique there are as many factors as variables.

Such a solution, and indeed any other first solution, is a description of the data in terms of factors or dimensions. It states that the correlations can be accounted for by X factors with the loadings as calculated. In a complex factor analysis, examination of the factor loadings usually fails to reveal the psychological nature of the factors. In any case, since there is an infinity of solutions, even if the first solution makes sense, how do we know it is the best solution? Thurstone (1947) proposed that *rotation to simple structure* solved the problem, a view powerfully supported by Cattell (e.g. 1978). This must now be explicated.

Factors as vectors

Factors can be regarded as vectors in factor space. The infinity of possible solutions derives from the fact that there is no method of fixing the position of these axes absolutely; it can be done relatively, the only constraint being that the cross-multiplication of the loadings can reproduce the original correlations.

Simple structure, as defined by Thurstone (1947), aimed to rotate the vectors to a position relative to each other such that each factor had a few high loadings and a large number of low or nil loadings. This makes each factor simple to interpret, hence the name. The rationale of simple structure is the law of parsimony, Occam's razor: each factor-analytic solution can be regarded as a hypothesis accounting for the correlations, and thus the simplest is to be preferred. In addition, simple-structure solutions are usually replicable (Cattell, 1978). We must now examine the problems involved in attaining simple structure.

Rotation to simple structure

To enable the reader to grasp the problems of rotation to simple structure, a few further technical terms must be defined.

Orthogonal factors and orthogonal rotation   If the factors in the rotation are kept at right angles (orthogonal) to each other, then the factors are themselves uncorrelated, for the cosine of the angle between the vectors indicates the correlation between the factors.

Oblique factors and oblique rotations   In oblique rotation the angles between the vectors can be of any size, so that they can take up the position yielding the simplest structure as defined by Thurstone. Since the cosine of the angle between the vectors indicates the correlation between them, oblique factors are correlated.

Higher-order factors

In any large-scale study with a considerable number of oblique factors, it is possible to factor analyse the correlations between the factors: this results in second-order factors. The correlations between these can be factored, resulting in third orders and so on, until at last only one or two orthogonal factors emerge. Thus primary factors load on the original test variables, second-orders load on primary factors and third-orders on second-orders. Higher-order factors are thus likely to be very broad, fundamental concepts.

In practice, it seems likely that with real-life, complex data, factors, being underlying dimensions, would be correlated. Furthermore, oblique factoring allows the best position to be taken up on the criterion of simple structure as defined by Thurstone. This is Cattell's view. Guilford, on the other hand, claims that orthogonal factors are by definition more simple than oblique, hence he prefers that method (e.g. Guilford and Hoepfner, 1971). Our view is that in the highly complicated field of personality, it is indeed likely that oblique factors will be required to fit the data and that therefore oblique solutions are to be favoured. However, Barrett and Kline (1980) attained an ideal solution to this problem, in that an oblique rotation procedure, direct oblimin, was modified such that if the best simple structure was in fact orthogonal, an orthogonal position could be reached.

In summary, therefore, there is a simple argument to counter the objection to factor analysis that there is an infinity of solutions. Rotation to simple structure, as defined by Thurstone, provides us with the most parsimonious (and therefore preferred) solution. Such simple-structure solutions are also replicable. Usually an oblique-factor structure best fits the data, and this can yield high-order factors of even greater simplicity, factors of considerable breadth. Thus what is to be aimed for in factor analyses is clear, simple structure solutions, elegant and parsimonious and replicable.

All this must make readers wonder why there are any problems with factor analyses. Unfortunately, these principles are difficult to put into practice. Cattell (1978) and Cattell and Kline (1977) have shown that many published factor analyses cannot be taken at face value because technical deficiencies have resulted in artefacts obscuring the results. In addition, Nunnally (1978) has clearly demonstrated the statistical need for adequate factor analyses. Here we shall deliberately restrict our discussion to the technical needs for adequate analyses as they affect the construction of personality tests.

1 If we are trying to develop a test of extraversion all the elements in the syndrome must be sampled (i.e. there must be items relevant to all traits); otherwise any resulting factor is bound to be defective.

2 If we are attempting to develop a test of psychoticism, a variable higher in abnormal than normal groups, then we must sample some abnormals, otherwise low variance among normals can lead to the factor's failure to emerge, as occurred in the work of Helmes (1980) and Loo (1979) on the EPQ, a technical difficulty which led them to incorrect conclusions (see Barrett and Kline, 1981a).

3 It is generally agreed that samples of less than 200 can lead to variations in factor structure (see Guilford, 1956). Certainly, samples of less than 100 are unlikely to yield reliable results. If samples are small, results should always be replicated.

4 Guilford, for reasons of matrix algebra, advocates that there should always be at least twice as many subjects as variables. This is really the minimum figure, and Nunnally (1978) advocates a ratio of 10 to 1. Such a ratio makes the factor-analytic method difficult to use for large item pools. Nevertheless, the ratio of two to one should not be cut.

There is little doubt that the number of factors rotated can signally affect the attainment of simple structure. Generally, it seems to be the case that with a large number of factors the scree test (Cattell, 1966) or the MAP test (Velicer, 1976) give similar and reliable results, as Barrett and Kline (1981b) have shown in an empirical study of the problem. One commonly used method of estimating significant factors, the Kaiser–Guttman (Kaiser, 1958), does not work well with large numbers of small factors such as are found in test construction; indeed, it was never designed so to do (Hakstian and Muller, 1973).

These are the most important requirements for technically adequate factor analyses, and with them in mind, together with our description of the nature of factors and rotation, we can now easily describe the factor-analytic method of test construction.

The factor-analytic method

In this items are intercorrelated and subjected to simple-structure factor analyses. Items loading on one factor only are selected for that scale. Items loading on no factors or on many factors are usually rejected. The rationale, of course, is that if a factor underlies a set of items, then they must be homogeneous. Such a method of test construction guarantees that the test is measuring only one variable (the factor) and that some dimension accounts for the variance. Of course, validity studies are necessary to identify the factor on which the items load.

The main difficulty with the method lies in the unreliability of the dichotomous item, which means that factors often account only for a small proportion of the test variance. In addition, the inter-item correlational index (e.g. *phi*), is affected by different item splits. Indeed, factoring can lead to difficulty factors emerging (e.g. Levy, 1973), to low correlations and subsequently rather unclear factor analyses. In addition, simple structure should clearly be reached, since obviously replicable results are essential.

Well-known tests constructed by these methods are Cattell's 16PF test, the EPQ constructed by Eysenck and Eysenck (1975) and the personality tests of Guilford and his colleagues.

Despite the fact that some of the best-known inventories are factor-analytic, some authorities, especially Nunnally (1978), believe that the practical problems are so great – especially the low variance of some items and, in his case, the necessity of having ten times more subjects than variables, which means a huge item trial, for the method demands many items – that it is better to use the analogous item-analytic method. Certainly, in his own test construction, the author found that factoring items failed to yield clear factors due to problems of item variability, different rates of item endorsement and the practical difficulties of obtaining sufficiently large test trial samples. Item-analytic methods were therefore used.

The item-analytic method

The standard item-analytic method of producing a homogeneous test is to correlate each item with the total score on the item pool or, if several scales are being constructed simultaneously, to correlate each item with their total scale score. The point-biserial correlation is used, and items correlating significantly with the total (preferably beyond 0.3), and with endorsement rates within the 80–20 per cent band, are chosen. Since each item correlates with the total, a homogeneous test must thus be produced, and the limitations on the facility value of 80–20 per cent ensure that it is reasonably discriminating. As with the factorial method, replication on several samples means that item variability does not cause a bad item to be chosen. The validity of such a scale (i.e. the identification of the underlying variable) must then be demonstrated.

This approach has its rationale in the classical model of error variance which we have described above. As we have argued, it is easier to produce item-analytically successful scales than factorial scales: item variability destroys results to a lesser extent and smaller samples are adequate. Studies of the EPQ show that the results of the two types of analysis, where both work, are highly similar (Barrett and Kline, 1980). Provided that the factorial nature of the test variable is identified by factoring the scale score with other relevant scales (in validity studies), this method is satisfactory and practicable without the expenditure of prodigious research time. Its major disadvantage is the fact that the item-analytic method can produce a scale that is multifactorial if the factors are highly correlated. The item analysis will select items loading on such factors. However, subsequent factor analysis of the scales would reveal this fact. In brief, this is a practicable method for producing personality inventories where research time and money are limited. Where they are not, factor analysis is probably to be preferred, but there is little essential difference between the methods.

Such, then, are the principles of personality inventory construction. To conclude our chapter, we shall list and briefly describe the best-known personality tests. From some of these have been obtained the data, to be discussed in later sections of this book, which in our view should form the basis of fully scientific theories of personality.

Table 1 *Some personality tests**

Test	Method of construction	Number and type of items	Variables measured and other comments
Ai3Q (Kline, 1971)	Item analysis	30 items: yes/no	Useful for testing psycho-analytic theory. Measures anal or obsessional character
Californian Psychological Inventory (Gough, 1975)	Criterion-keyed	480 items: true/false	18 scales (e.g. dominance, sociability, achievement). The sane man's MMPI
Comrey Personality Scales (Comrey, 1970)	Factor analysis of item clusters	180 items: with rating scales	10 factors: trust, orderliness, conformity, activity, stability, extra-version, masculinity and empathy, + 2 validity checks
Dynamic Personality Inventory (Grygier, 1961)	Factor analysis of scales and item analysis	336 items: list of words subjects indicate like/dislike	33 scales measuring psychoanalytic psychosexual variables. Measures different variables from EPQ and 16 PF tests
Edwards Personal Preference Schedule (Edwards, 1959)	Item analyses of scales	Forced-choice items to eliminate social desirability; ipsative scoring (i.e. scores are related to each other)	Based upon Murray (1938). Measures 15 of Murray's needs

* Widely used, interesting or the author's own.

Table 1 *Some personality tests*

Test	Method of construction	Number and type of items	Variables measured and other comments
The Eysenck Personality Questionnaire (Eysenck and Eysenck, 1975)	Factor analysis of items: canonical analysis	98 items: yes/no	Extraversion, neuroticism, psychoticism are measured in this scale. Very clear factor structure
Guilford–Zimmerman Temperament Survey (Guilford and Zimmerman, 1949)	Factor analysis of items for most scales	300 items: yes/no	10 orthogonal factors: activity, restraint, ascendance, sociability, stability, objectivity, friendliness, thoughtfulness, personal relations and masculinity
The Minnesota Multiphasic Personality Inventory	Criterion-keyed scales	558 items: true/false	9 clinical scales, more than 200 empirically derived scales, and 6000 references. Hypochondriasis, depression, hysteria, introversion, psychopathy, masculinity, paranoia, psychasthenia, schizophrenia and mania

Table 1   *Some personality tests*

Test	Method of construction	Number and type of items	Variables measured and other comments
The Myers–Briggs Inventory (Briggs and Myers, 1962)	Item analysis	Various kinds of item	Measures Jungian personality variables. Thinking, feeling, sensory and intuiting introversion, extraversion
The Personality Research Form (Jackson, 1974)	Item analysis	300 items	2 forms: measuring 15 or 22 of Murray's (1938) needs. Item analysis of exceptional detail and scope
16PF Test (Cattell *et al.*, 1970a)	Factor analysis	187 items: trichotomous and forced-choice	Measures the 16 factors claimed to be the most important in the personality sphere. Very considerable body of knowledge has been accumulated concerning the factors. Versions for children of 4 years up to adults
OOQ and OPQ (Kline, 1980a)	Item analysis	20 items in each test: yes/no	Measures oral-optimistic and oral-pessimistic character, as described by Freud

These tests constitute some of the most widely used personality inventories. The Comrey, Guilford, Eysenck and Cattell tests from the major factor-analytic essays into personality structure, and the results of these and their implications for a theoretical understanding of personality, will be discussed fully later in this book. The MMPI, CPI and PRF represent the most powerful attempts to measure personality variables utilizing the non-theoretical, criterion-keyed approach. The other tests included in this list are either essentially exercises in test construction (e.g. the EPPS) or attempts to use tests to investigate particular psychoanalytic theories (theories which prejudiced experimentalists have labelled untestable).

The descriptions are necessarily brief. They are intended to give readers an analytic and easily comparable picture of what inventories are like. These tests (with the exception of the author's own and perhaps the DPI) are generally regarded as among the best inventories, as evidenced by the reviews of Buros (1978, for example). For full descriptions and critical discussions, readers must be referred to the *Mental Measurement Yearbooks*. Most personality tests, as readers of Buros will discover, are very poor, unreliable and of unknown validity, with poor norms and with no real rationale. However, our list is not exhaustive; just because a test is not listed we do not necessarily imply that it is no good. However, we have inserted what we consider to be the best tests.

Summary

The following topics were described, discussed and evaluated:

1 Different types of personality inventory item
2 The provenance of item pools
3 Methods of test construction
   (a) criterion-keyed methods
   (b) a description of factor analysis
   (c) factor-analytic methods
   (d) item-analytic methods
4 Some well-known tests

4 Psychological tests of personality 2: projective tests

Projective tests were briefly, if somewhat loosely, described as ambiguous stimuli to which subjects are required to respond. In fact, Semeonoff (1973, 1977), in his excellent surveys of projective testing, has developed a very useful classificatory system for projective tests which enables one to see how projective measures relate to each other.

In essence, Semeonoff (1973) classifies projective stimuli thus: (1) verbal, (2) visual, (3) other sense modalities, (4) concrete. Projective responses may be also classified: (1) description, (2) classification or diagnosis, (3) therapy. This classification not only allows one to see how different techniques are related to each other, but it is also valuable for developing new methods, although some combinations may not be particularly useful. This classification, however, makes abundantly clear what a projective test is and hence is effectively a definition.

The tests: objections and a defence

The objections to projective tests, made with typical ferocity by Eysenck (1959) and summarized more soberly by Vernon (1964), are so well made that they can be simply listed. Basically, the following flaws can be said to vitiate projective tests.

1 There is no adequate theory to account for claims that the responses to projective tests tap a subject's idiodynamics. The notion of projection as used in projective tests is quite different from the Freudian defence mechanism (not that this would any longer confer any scientific respectability – quite the opposite, indeed).
2 The reliability of projective test scoring is not high. This is due to differences between different occasions with the same scorer.
3 As is to be expected in the light of 2, studies of the validity of projective tests are not encouraging; the more rigorously the validity studies are executed, the lower the validity coefficients that emerge.

4   Many projective tests, especially the Rorschach, claim to measure a large number of variables. This in itself distinguishes them from most measures used in other sciences, which, like the unifactorial scales advocated in Chapter 3, measure one variable only.

5   As Vernon (1964) points out, a number of extraneous variables have been shown to affect projective test results, which is odd if these tests do measure the deeper layers of personality. Examples of such variables are the mood of the subject, the mood of the tester, the attitude of the subject to the test, what he thinks the test is about, the attitude of the tester and, in the case of blacks and whites in America, the race of the tester.

In the light of these problems and difficulties, many psychologists have abandoned projective testing as a method of gathering worthwhile scientific data, and indeed in his studies of the scientific validity of Freudian theory (Kline, 1973a, 1981) the present author has maintained this viewpoint. There seems little doubt that standard interpretations of projective test responses are likely to be riddled with error.

Consequently, there arises the serious question of the reasons for bothering at all with projective tests, given the basic correctness of the objections. Yet there are two points that need raising in defence of projective tests, the second of which clearly supports their continued use.

The first point concerns the method used by academic psychologists to investigate the validity of projective tests. The usual method (e.g. Eysenck, 1959) is to have raters rate protocols blind (i.e. with no knowledge of the subject). Although this appears to be a fair test, in fact it is rather absurd, and no one in his right mind would attempt to evaluate a projective test response without taking the subject into account. For example, a protocol with great emphasis on bananas would surely be different in meaning if it was the product of a young girl in love for the first time or of a monkey keeper at a zoo. Just as the psychoanalysis of dreams has to be undertaken in the context of the subject's life, so too does the interpretation of projective test protocols. From this we may conclude that such demonstrations of invalidity are not as devastating as they first appear.

The second counter is much more powerful and, in our view, makes the continued use of projective tests possible. Since the basic objection to projective tests concerns the unreliability of scoring and interpretation, an obvious approach is to develop a method for objective, reliable scoring and analysis. In fact, an objective method of this kind has been developed for the Rorschach by Holley (1973) – G analysis, which has also been used with other tests by the present author (Hampson and Kline, 1977).

G analysis

Holley (1973) described in detail the G analysis of some Rorschach protocols of depressives, schizophrenics and controls. The results, which were cross-validated on different samples, showed a striking discrimination between these three groups. Holley concluded both that the findings lent support to the claims of clinicians concerning the Rorschach and that it was a powerful personality test. He attributed the failure of previous academic studies of the Rorschach to demonstrate validity to the impropriety of their statistical methods.

Since this 1973 paper Holley and his co-workers, especially Vegelius (1976), have considerably expanded the scope of G analysis and have shown it to be effective with other groups, as have Hampson and Kline (1977). For our purposes we shall describe G analysis only in its most basic form, since it is perhaps the method of scoring rather than the statistical aspect of the technique that is most important.

The following steps are involved in G analysis:

1 objectively scoring the projective test protocols;
2 correlating people (on the basis of the projective test scores) by means of the G index;
3 factoring the correlations between people and thus forming groups – Q-factor analysis;
4 finding what variables discriminate the groups.

Objectively scoring the protocols

As we have indicated, this may be the most crucial aspect of G analysis. Certainly, Kline and Svaste-Xuto (1981), who used the scoring procedure but analysed the scores with simple *chi*-squares, were able to find psychologically significant results. We shall therefore concentrate on describing the scoring procedures.

The protocols of each subject are scored for the presence or absence of variables. Two examples will clarify the point. Let us suppose we have the drawings of a house of subjects A and B, as part of the House Tree Person Test (Buck, 1970). Subject A has drawn a large house with roof, tiles, three chimneys, windows, curtains, a door with a large door knob. Subject B has drawn a small thatched cottage. The door and window are open; there is no chimney; and a complex garden path leads to the door. The following variables would be used (0 indicates that the subject did not score on them, 1 that he did). Size is arbitrarily decided by the proportion of paper used in the drawing of the particular object.

Variables	Large house	Small house	Roof	Tiles	Thatch	None	Chimneys 1	2	3
Subject A	1	0	1	1	0	0	0	0	1
Subject B	0	1	1	0	1	1	0	0	0

Variables	Windows	Windows open	Curtains	Door	Door open	Door knob	Path straight	Path curved
Subject A	1	0	1	1	0	1	0	0
Subject B	1	1	0	1	1	0	0	1

As this example shows, the protocols of subjects may be encapsulated with as much detail as the investigator has patience. Each new subject will be likely to require new variables on which previous subjects scored 0. Projective tests of all kinds, interviews and responses to questions about the tests can be scored in this way.

This, of course, results in a very large number of variables, and it is usually necessary to remove variables on which fewer than five subjects score because otherwise there will be artefactually high correlations between subjects (alike because they didn't give idiosyncratic responses).

Correlating the subjects

Clearly, the statistical analysis chosen must depend on the aim of the testing, the hypothesis under investigation. However, in the psycho-metric approach to personality the object is often to be able to discriminate groups, and here the G analysis to be described is entirely appropriate. We shall exemplify the method (although this was not, in fact, used) from the study by Kline and Svaste-Xuto (1981), where an attempt was made to differentiate between Thai, British and American 4-year-olds who used the HTP test and the CAT (Bellak, Bellak and Haworth, 1974).

People (not variables) are correlated using the G index of

agreement (Holley and Guilford, 1964). The formula for G is G = $2Pc-1$ where Pc is the number of agreements in a contingency table. G is, therefore, like $\emptyset$ and tetrachoric r, a correlation coefficient for dichotomous data. However, unlike these coefficients, it is not affected by differing proportions in the splits of item responses or by the way the item happens to be scored – that is, whether a roof is scored 0 or 1, which, of course, is arbitrary; we could as easily have had a variable 'no roof', and subjects A and B would then have scored 0. It is to be noted that G is most useful in correlating persons. In correlating variables it can give rise to factors based upon the difficulty level of items (i.e. the split of responses). Thus a factor might emerge based on all items with a 35–65 response split.

From correlating subjects we arrive at a correlation matrix of subjects based upon their responses to the projective tests. In our example, therefore, we had the correlations between British, American and Thai children on the HTP and CAT tests. This must now be subjected to factor analysis.

Factoring the subjects

In factoring subjects the resulting factors load on people. Thus if factor 1 loads on subjects A, B and E, then these three form a group. Such factoring is known as Q-factor analysis. Clearly, then, in our example we would hope to obtain factors loading on Thai children, thus showing them as distinct from British and American controls on the tests. The factor analysis proceeds as described in Chapter 4, the aim being to reach simple structure. Orthogonal rotations are simpler to interpret, since the meaning of correlated groups is not obvious.

If we find clear factors – factors with high loadings on subjects and with each subject loading only on one factor (i.e. a member of only one group) – then effectively we have discriminated between the groups of subjects on the projective tests. The final step is to discover the variables which bring about this discrimination.

Finding the discriminating variables

Holley (1973) suggests that this be done by a simple frequency-based statistic – the D estimate. This is fine where the factors form clear groups, but where this is not the case, as with bipolar factors, D estimates can sometimes give variable results. In addition, the significance of D estimates is unknown. Factor scores may be a way round this difficulty. With this computation we now have the variables discriminating the groups.

Although, since the publication of the 1973 paper Holley and his colleagues have considerably developed G analysis – for example, it is now usable with trichotomous data (see Holley, 1975), and weighted indices are possible to increase discrimination (Vegelius, 1976) – the basic approach described above certainly enables projective-test material to be submitted to rigorous statistical analysis, and powerful discrimination is now possible. In Chapter 10 we shall discuss some of this work, but here it is sufficient to point out as evidence of the utility of the method the fact that various clear results have been found – for example, high discrimination among clinical groups (Schubo *et al.*, 1975) and among two kinds of murderer (Hampson, 1975).

Conclusions

In our view, G analysis does allow projective tests to be used in the quantitative study of personality. Since it is clear that projective tests can tap a rich source of data, this is particularly important. Effectively it means that the intuitive judgements of clinicians can be quantified, and if found valuable, used.

Before leaving the topic, however, a few cautionary notes should be sounded. First, the statistical analysis itself, although efficient, is not the only way in which to analyse the data. A discriminant function analysis, for example, might prove just as efficient. Second, our own studies of criminals (Hampson and Kline, 1977), although they produced good discriminations, did not produce replicated factors; the factors were different for each sample, defining the factors by the discriminating variables. Whether this was a genuine sample difference or not cannot be ascertained. Despite these warnings, G analysis does seem to offer a method of utilizing the rich data of projective tests. Hence we shall not abandon them.

The best-known and some interesting projective tests: brief descriptions

The Rorschach Test (Rorschach, 1921)

This is indubitably *the* psychological test, consisting of ten symmetrical ink blots which subjects are asked, in essence, to describe. Scoring, and especially interpretation, are highly skilled tasks and require lengthy training. With over 5000 references in papers and dissertations, there is a large body of research findings relating Rorschach scores to mainly clinical phenomena, although, as Eysenck (1959) has argued, the scientific rigour of much of this work is not notable. Two detailed scoring systems have been developed, that of Beck (1952) and that of Klopfer *et al.* (1956). Our interest in this test derives from the spectacular results achieved by the Lund group working with Holley (1973) and using G analysis rather than the standard interpretative system, which is highly subjective.

It should be noted that Holtzman (1968) has produced a version of the Rorschach with forty blots, which are described by multiple-choice options and thus render the test reliable. However, inevitably much of the typical richness of Rorschach protocols is lost. This may be abandoning validity for the sake of reliability.

The Thematic Apperception Test (Murray, 1938)

This projective test is a series of ambiguous pictures, mainly of human beings, which subjects are asked to describe. Murray developed a scoring system to measure the needs and presses considered in his personology to be the most important determinants of human behaviour. The notion of needs has proved intuitively appealing to test constructors, since, it will be remembered (see Chapter 3), both Edwards and Jackson produced inventories purporting to measure these needs despite the lack of any firm empirical evidence in their support.

Murstein (1963) contains much useful information showing that the TAT can be scored to measure a large variety of variables. Many of the scoring schemes have been constructed empirically according to the ability of the scores to discriminate between various groups, although the scientific rigour of the studies is, as was the case with the Rorschach, not impressive. However, some special reliable scoring schemes for the TAT have been developed (see Zubin *et al.*, 1966), and it is probable that this test could be used to yield useful quantitative data, although as yet this has not been achieved.

If one is prepared to accept that projective testing can be valuable – and many clinically oriented psychologists do believe this and would regard the quantitative approach advocated here to be unnecessary and bad, in that nuances of meaning are inevitably lost – then the TAT, like the Rorschach, is a test of huge potential. Because of this a number of variants have been developed, of which two deserve brief mention.

Bellak, Bellak and Haworth (1974) have produced a children's TAT, the CAT, which shows children in a variety of family scenes that are thought to be important in analytically oriented child psychology. There is also an animal version because some children, according to the authors, identify more easily with animals than with humans. It must be pointed out the CAT has a basically psychoanalytic rather than a personological rationale.

The other interesting variant was an African version of the TAT constructed by Lee (1953) for pan-cultural use. This proved usable only for the limited part of Africa where it was developed, so that its value is potential rather than actual. However, the construction of a thoroughly pan-cultural test (Price-Williams, 1965) remains a fascinating challenge.

As we found with personality inventories, an examination of the huge number of projective tests shows that most of them are woefully short of evidence for reliability and validity and their rationale is little more than the unique clinical intuition of their authors. However, a small number of tests have some research evidence to back their claims, and the data from these tests, if reliably scored and subjected to proper statistical analysis, deserve scrutiny.

The House Tree Person Test (Buck, 1948)

In the HTP subjects draw a house, a tree and a person and answer certain questions about their drawings. A considerable weight of clinical research has been gathered into two manuals (Buck, 1948; Buck, 1970). These clinical data, brilliant speculations and deductions, if supported by sound quantified evidence, would render the HTP a valuable test. In fact, Hampson and Kline (1977), using G analysis with criminals, and Kline and Svaste-Xuto (1981), using an objective scoring scheme with 4-year-old Thai children, have supported some of the claims in the manual. There is little doubt that the HTP could be a useful test.

The Blacky Pictures (Blum, 1949)

This is a particularly interesting test because the pictures (dogs in various family scenes) were designed to tap specific psychoanalytic psychosexual developmental stages. Descriptions reveal to what extent a subject is fixated at different psychosexual levels. Part of this test is objectively scored, and there is some evidence, fully reviewed by Kline (1972, 1973a, 1981), that this test has certain valid indices. Certainly, it deserves fully objective investigation.

Corman has developed what he considers to be an improved version of the Blacky Pictures, the Patte Noire Test, portraying a family of pigs (Corman, 1969). The pictures are less crude than the cartoon figures of the Blum Test, and the administration is more flexible. In addition, measures of defence mechanisms can be obtained, as well as other less specifically psychoanalytic data. Interpretation and scoring are entirely subjective, however.

Corman (1967) has also invented Le Gribouillis, the scribble test. A test mainly for children, it requires them to scribble and write their names. From the position of the scribble, inferences are made concerning personality development. This test is thus objective. Without strong evidence of validity, it deserves investigation, for Corman, as the manuals to his tests make clear, is indeed an imaginative clinician.

These last tests are interesting because they have been designed to test psychoanalytic hypotheses which, except to the prejudiced, are among the most stimulating in the field of personality.

This brief list of projective tests typifies the genre, and we shall include no further examples. For other varieties readers are referred to Semeonoff (1977).

Before leaving the topic of projective tests, we want to discuss a final measure, the Defence Mechanism Test (Kragh, 1969; Kragh and Smith, 1970), together with its rationale, which is quite different from that of other projective tests.

The Defence Mechanism Test (DMT)

Description of the test　The DMT consists of two pictures, differing in detail and containing three elements: the hero, who is the central figure, a boy or girl, a young man or a woman; the hero's attribute, a gun, car or violin; and a threat figure, a man or woman with a fierce face. There are parallel forms of the two pictures with males or females for each sex respectively.

Presentation of pictures　These pictures are presented tachisto-scopically with serially increasing exposure times, beginning below the threshold of awareness and continuing to full recognition. Kragh (1955) states, given a fixed ambient light, the geometric progression of exposure times.

Responses of subjects   For each successive exposure subjects draw and describe what they saw.

Variables claimed to be measured   Essentially, it is claimed by Kragh (1955) that changes in description as the scenes progress reveal defences: repression, isolation, denial, reaction formation, identification with the aggressor, turning against self.

Theoretical rationale of the test   The theoretical rationale of this test is to be found in percept-genetics, an aspect of psychology which is little studied beyond the universities of Lund and Oslo. Percept-genetic theory is so complex that a bare summary alone is possible here. Full descriptions can be found in Kragh (1955), Kragh (1969), Kragh and Smith (1970), Sjoback (1967) and Westerlundh (1976). A detailed summary is contained in Kline (1980c).

The name percept-genetics reflects the fact that the theory is concerned with how perception is built up (i.e. its genesis). Perception is regarded as a process that takes place between an individual and the stimulus. In normal, everyday perception this constructive process is automatic and virtually instantaneous. However, the serial tachistoscopic presentation of the DMT fragments the stimulus, thus allowing the interactive process between the individual and his world to be observed.

According to percept-genetic theory, study of these perceptual processes reveals information concerning an individual's personality – defence mechanisms (the way threats are coped with), together with drives and material associated with drives. In addition, life events of crucial emotional significance are also uncovered.

Kragh and Smith (1970), in their collection of papers on percept-genetics, try to demonstrate these claims from their empirical studies and also attempt to show that the DMT can differentiate nosological groups in accordance with psychoanalytic and general clinical theory.

Certainly, examination of some of the presented protocols does seem to show clear defence mechanisms, as indeed Kline and Cooper (1977) found, using a pig as a stimulus. The claim that there is a parallelism between real-life events and material emerging at different points in the serial presentation is far more difficult to accept, however, although in some instances this may be so.

At present there is no unequivocal evidence for the validity of the DMT as a measure of defences, although there is a wealth of interesting and convincing clinical material. Furthermore, it does seem that the variables can differentiate occupational and psychiatric groups, results which will be discussed in later chapters of this book. As for its ability to uncover critical life events, far more research is necessary before this claim can be verified. There is little doubt, however, that the DMT is a test which deserves full investigation to discover its merits and limitations. Of all projective techniques, it appears to be perhaps the most promising.

Summary

1 Projective tests were defined and categorized.
2 The problems described by academic psychologists were discussed, and suggestions as to how they could be countered were made.
3 G analysis was described, a powerful method of scoring and analysing projective tests.
4 Brief descriptions of some of the best-known and most useful projective tests were given: the Rorschach, the TAT, the CAT, the HTP, the Blacky Pictures, the PN, Le Gribouillis.
5 Finally, the DMT was described, and its rationale in percept-genetics was discussed.

5 Psychological tests of personality 3: objective personality tests

Objective tests, as we saw in Chapter 2, were defined, following Cattell (e.g. 1957), as tests which could be objectively scored and whose meaning was hidden from subjects. Underlying the objective test is the implicit assumption that since personality is the sum total of behaviour, then all differences in behaviour should in some way reflect differences in personality. Objective tests are, therefore, essentially measures of individual differences in behaviour. They are regarded by Cattell as the best method of personality measurement, although as yet there are few published test batteries and even fewer studies which yield convincing evidence for the validity of any of these objective (T) factors.

The construction and rationale of objective tests

The first obvious question in respect of the rationale of objective tests concerns their nature: what constitutes an objective test? After all, there would appear to be an infinite number of tasks that could be scored objectively, and certainly nobody could guess their purpose.

Hundleby (1973) has classified all personality tests in such a way that some essential features of objective tests are revealed. Among his categories those that would embrace objective tests are expressive movement (graphology is a well-known example of such a test), simulated real-life situations, physiological variables, motor-perceptual and performance tests. This last category includes the majority of objective-test devices; Cronbach uses the term 'performance tests' rather than objective tests in his (1970) textbook.

The importance of these categories to the constructor of objective tests is that they suggest that a good battery of such measures should contain tests from each category in order to minimize the importance of the variance that is specific to each category. For example, if we use questionnaires alone, as we saw in our discussion of these tests, we obtain variance due to the response sets of acquiescence and social desirability, together with variance attributable to using a particular kind of item. Fiske (1971) refers to this as 'method' variance; Cattell calls it 'instrument' variance (e.g. Cattell and Kline, 1977).

A second feature of this classification system is that quite clearly projective tests, given objective scoring and the fact that they are not too obvious, fall into the last category of performance tests.

However, from our viewpoint, that of trying to grasp the rationale of objective tests, there is one weakness in Hundleby's classification. It is that most such measures simply fall into the last umbrella category, so that the original problem remains: how do we choose a test from the huge range of performance tests?

First, as Cattell makes clear (Cattell and Kline, 1977), Cattell and colleagues used their clinical intuition. If some behaviour was thought to reflect a personality trait, it was translated into a test. An easy example was handwriting pressure. Observation suggests that tense people press hard when writing, in contrast to relaxed, easy-going subjects. A handwriting pressure test was therefore developed.

However, clinical intuition alone is not sufficient: what is necessary is some definition of the population of possible tests so that a reasonable sample can be constructed. Cattell and Warburton (1965), whose compendium of objective tests includes about 800 devices, did construct a taxonomy of objective tests to aid construction:

Dimensions	*Parameters*
1 Instructions	Reacting v. not reacting, ordered v. unordered response
2 Situations	Restricted v. unrestricted response, inventive v. selective answer, homogeneous v. patterned
3 Mode of response	Objective v. distortable, overt v. physiological
4 Mode of scoring	Normative v. ipsative

These are the most important dimensions and their associated parameters. As was the case with the taxonomy of projective tests discussed in the last chapter, this taxonomy allows one to locate tests in relation to other objective tests and to develop new ones. For example, by looking at the taxonomy we could try to develop tests where the parameter involved was reacting v. non-reacting and scoring was physiological. Immediately we can think of taste tests of various chemicals, measuring saliva flow.

Hundleby's taxonomy, on the other hand, enables us to locate objective tests in relation to other tests of personality. With these two systems in mind, it is now possible to grasp the rationale of objective tests. Some examples should clarify the argument.

Some possible objective tests: their rationale and their place in the taxonomies

Expressive movements (first extensively studied by Allport and Vernon, 1933) comprise the first of Hundleby's categories of objective tests. There is no doubt that these are regarded as powerful indices of personality in psychological folklore. Hearty laughing, bouncy walking, shifty looking, straight-between-the-eyes looking, small handwriting, large handwriting – all exemplify simply interpreted behaviours. These could be tried out as measures of personality if reliable scoring indices could be used. Writing too has the added problem that it is affected by variables such as how often we write and how we were taught. We agree with Hundleby's conclusions concerning expressive movement: that it is worth trying as an objective test of personality and that it probably taps some personality variance, although clearly not all.

The simulated real-life situation (Hundleby's second category) was used extensively in wartime for officer selection. For example, a discussion group might be organized at which a decision had to be made about which of two plans was the better. Objective test scores (e.g. number of interruptions, length of time spent speaking, number of adjectives per sentence, number of times ideas were accepted) could be derived from this. Notice that if this exercise were merely rated by judges as revealing verbal ability, logical deduction or persuasibility, it would no longer be an objective test. Such simulations can be useful tests for occupational psychology, where simulations are easier to develop than in the purely psychological measurement of personality. Of course, the validity of such tests as these has to be demonstrated.

Hundleby's third category of physiological tests, physiological indices, is represented as yet by few examples in objective testing, although if Eysenck's (1967) theorizing concerning the nature of N, E and P, as reflecting variations in autonomic nervous activity, central nervous arousal and androgen level respectively, is correct, such tests should be powerful. Heart rate, EEG and GSR are typical physiological tests, although their factorial composition is not clear.

Since they need laboratory facilities for testing, their practical value in applied psychology is limited.

This discussion makes it clear that most objective tests must fall into Hundleby's fourth category of motor-perceptual and performance tests. This is the point where Cattell and Warburton's (1965) taxonomy of instructions, situations, modes of response and modes of survey becomes useful, since it is to this fourth domain of tests that the taxonomy is most appropriate.

Motor-perceptual performance tests

As we have argued, the major problem here concerns the almost infinite number of possible tests, a problem further compounded because, virtually by definition, objective tests are not face-valid: if they were, their purport could be guessed. This not only renders test construction difficult, but it also makes the demonstration of validity essential.

Apart from clinical intuition, therefore, which we have already mentioned, Cattell and colleagues have used their taxonomy to develop as wide a variety of tests as possible, with the aim of covering the whole population of possible objective tests and of minimizing the effects of specific test variance.

In Cattell and Warburton (1965) 800 devices are listed that are constructed on the principles described above, devices yielding more than 2000 variables. Each test is described, and its factor loadings are quoted, followed where possible by an interpretation. For the full range of objective tests readers must refer to the compendium. What we shall do here is to describe and discuss a small sample of these tests, concentrating on those which load on the best-known factors and on the few published batteries, for it must be realized that most of these objective tests are suitable as yet only for research.

The tests we shall describe have been especially selected as typical of objective devices after consultation with Professor Cattell and have been described in Cattell and Kline (1977).

T42 mazes   This test loads highest on the largest objective test factor – assertive ego. There are four mazes which subjects traverse as quickly as possible with a pencil, without touching the sides; fifteen seconds is the time limit for each maze. From this simple device the following variables may be extracted: (a) absolute speed; (b) accuracy; (c) accuracy relative to speed; (d) distance covered; (e) relative speed on the more difficult mazes.

T45 line-length judgement   Pairs of lines are presented to subjects, who have to judge whether they are the same length or whether one of the pair is the longer, the majority being so similar that there is a genuine difficulty in deciding. The score used is the number of pairs attempted. There are two points worthy of note in respect of this test, both of which contribute to our understanding of the nature of objective tests. First, subjects really have no way of faking this test. At best, one could sabotage it. Second, for almost all subjects the judgement required is so simple (one of length) that it is reasonable to regard the measure as one of natural temperamental speed. Recent work by Brand (1980) suggests that this test may measure intelligence.

T314 Heartogram   This test exemplifies the objective physiological test. The Heartogram is a machine for measuring the increase in heart rate after the subject has been startled. It would not be useful for selection purposes other than in very large and wealthy organizations, since it requires laboratory facilities and is an individual not a group test.

T42 and 45 are simple pencil-and-paper objective tests. T314 is a laboratory physiological measure. However, if we scrutinize just the tests loading on the largest objective test factor, we can see a great variety. We shall examine some of these.

Highbrow tastes   This seems a rather weak measure, comparing good, informed taste with ignorant, uneducated taste in a diverse number of fields – music, the arts, dress and drama, for example. Subjects have to state preference for canasta, bridge or poker, ballet, a musical or a Western. Cattell and Warburton (1965) argue that its loading on U.1.16 assertiveness can be interpreted as showing that highbrow tastes have their origins in competitiveness and variety. This item we deemed weak because while this may be so in the American sample, it may equally not be so in Britain and Europe, where the status of the intellectual is quite different. In any case, objective tests should be more culture-free than questionnaires. This test is not likely to be successful in this respect, since the items are most clearly culture-bound. Indeed, doubts could be raised about whether this questionnaire test is truly objective, since its purport, selecting the highbrow, does seem obvious.

Masculinity of interests This is another example of a questionnaire which is regarded as an objective test because its purpose, it is claimed by Cattell and Warburton, is hidden from subjects. It requires subjects to indicate their degree of satisfaction with their achievements in a number of fields, social, intellectual and academic. Certainly, few would be likely to guess that such a test measured masculinity of interests.

Backward reading For this test subjects read a story normally, then they are required to read it written backwards. The score obtained is the difference in the times for the two readings. This, therefore, is clearly quite objective. Few could guess how it is scored, and if they could, who would willingly distort his or her score? It is probable that rigid, inflexible people will read backwards relatively very slowly.

Reaction to social pressure on attitudes In this objective device ordinary attitude tests are used. However, their scoring and administration is far from usual. After the attitude test is completed, the attitudes of (a) authorities or (b) the majority are fed back to the subjects, who are later retested. The objective-test score is the shift in attitudes after this new information. Another form of the test involves new factual information about the relevant topics being fed to subjects. Change is again measured here, as a test of adaptability. This is indeed a subtle objective test.

There are a number of other group objective tests which have the superficial appearance of inventories or questionnaires but are in fact objective-test devices. One of these measures the exvia (Cattell's term for extraversion) factor. This consists of unqualified and carefully hedged statements. Subjects are asked to say with what statements they agree. Extraverts tend to choose the unqualified. Similarly, extraverts tend to agree with the majority view, as in the reaction to social pressures on attitudes test. Another questionnaire-like objective device counts the number of aphorisms checked as true, a test similar to those above.

Reaction-time tests In contrast to these questionnaire-like measures, the standard reaction timer, where buttons have to be pressed in response to visual or audible signals, is also used for objective personality testing, where the scores are the differences in response with different instructions and conditions – the number of failures to comply with instructions, the number of responses to the wrong stimulus, the ratio of reaction times on simple and complex responses. Clearly, this test is fully objective according to the criteria of the definition at the beginning of the chapter.

These tests illustrate the rich variety of objective-test devices, but they by no means constitute a perfect sample of the compendium, which is not possible in a short space. In our previous publication, *The Scientific Analysis of Personality and Motivation* (Cattell and Kline, 1977), where we attempted to summarize the huge corpus of Cattell's forty years of research into personality, we tabulated some sample test titles as a further indication of the variety of tests. With the permission of Academic Press this is reproduced below:

Willingness to play practical jokes
readiness to make an early decision while dark adaptation is proceeding
amplitude of voice under normal relative to delayed feedback conditions
awareness of social etiquette
basal metabolic rate
eidetic imagery
cancellation of letters (a vigilance task) compared under two conditions
readiness to imitate animal sounds
critical flicker fusion frequency
speed of arousal of negative after-images
preference for crayoning own rather than provided drawings
frequency of hand tremor in a decision situation
amount of laughter at jokes
pupil dilation after startle
more fidgeting while waiting as measured by the fidgetometer
   (a specially constructed chair with electrical contacts to record movement –
   a modern version of an invention by Galton)
speed of design copying
height of tower block construction (six year olds)
care in following detailed instructions
accuracy of gestalt completion
distance covered in a brass finger maze, with and without shock

So much for our examples of objective tests of personality. Clearly, they truly follow from our definition of personality as the sum total of behaviour. In essence, an objective test can be anything that gives rise to individual differences.

Our discussion and description of objective tests has been aimed at clarifying their rationale and illustrating their diversity. We shall now consider the advantages and disadvantages of objective tests compared with questionnaires and projective tests and then go on to describe the few published examples.

The advantages of objective tests

Resistance to faking

This is highly important where tests are used for selection. For example, what salesman applicant would admit that he was shy, didn't like meeting people and was easily persuaded of other people's point of view? As we have seen, in the main, objective tests cannot be faked because it is not clear what they measure or what score is going to be derived from the test.

Resistance to response sets

Those tests that are not of the questionnaire variety are unlikely to be affected by the response sets of social desirability or acquiescence, two major sources of measurement error in inventories. Of course, other response sets may conceivably affect the results, but if we use in our battery objective tests of many different kinds, as we have argued is desirable, the effect of any particular response set is minimal.

Resistance to self-illusion

Many subjects, although attempting to answer questionnaires as honestly as possible, have so many illusions concerning their feelings and behaviour that they might as well be deliberately lying. The present author has observed subjects responding 'Yes' to a question concerning whether they could quickly make decisions only after minutes of indecision and many alterations of the yes/no response. Eysenck too reports patients who are patently anxious, palpitating and perspiring, yet who claim on relevant items that they are not anxious. Obviously, objective tests of the non-questionnaire variety overcome this problem.

All these are important advantages compared with other personality tests, especially inventories. It is to be noted that projective tests or (if they cannot be guessed and can be objectively scored) objective tests are not free of social desirability. Thus in the Rorschach, for example, few normal people would report that an ink blot resembled a bloody murder, with the victim being sexually assaulted. However, most projective tests are more free than inventories of the problems discussed above, but care has to be taken in assessing the results and scores, especially while giving the test (by forming good rapport) to avoid the worst effects of social desirability.

Cattell (e.g. Cattell and Kline, 1977) claims another advantage for objective tests compared with inventories and projective tests. This is that objective tests are virtually culture-free and, even more important, time-free. For example, a personality-test item, or even (but to a lesser extent) a projective-test stimulus concerned with going to the cinema, is not only culture-bound but also time-bound. It is culture-bound because clearly the attitudes and notions of cinema-going differ from culture to culture, and many societies are fortunate enough to be innocent of cinema. It is time-bound even in a country like America or Britain because the status of the cinema in the hierarchy of entertainments has changed since the last war, greatly influenced, obviously, by the advent of television.

In fact, as Price-Williams (1961) has argued, and as is fully discussed in Chapter 11, it is exceedingly difficult to develop any kind of genuinely cross-cultural test. Projective tests are as embedded in the cultures in which they are developed as test items referring to culturally specific behaviours, even if less obviously. Furthermore, even items that appear to be applicable to two different cultures may, in fact, have different connotations in these cultures that render comparisons difficult. For example, in Ai3Q (Kline, 1971) there is an item concerned with dining out. This test was used in India, Africa and Britain, all countries where people dine out but in circumstances so different that cross-cultural comparison is probably absurd.

These arguments are probably applicable to objective tests. Obviously, questionnaire-type objective tests must suffer from dubious cultural applicability. However, even a test such as reaction time is likely to be affected by general cultural familiarity with technical apparatus involving buttons and lights. Most Westerners have similarly operated gadgets in their homes. The majority of Indians and Africans do not. Another example concerns the test preference for crayoning rather than drawing. It is highly likely that a variable such as this is strongly influenced by early experience with pencils and crayons and hence is not comparable across cultures. For all these reasons (and to some extent the same arguments apply to time), it cannot be assumed that objective tests will allow for cross-cultural comparison. Empirical studies are necessary, and as yet these have not been done. In summary, all one can say is that some major sources of cross-cultural bias are absent from objective tests but that freedom from cultural bias cannot be assumed.

The major difficulty with objective tests lies in establishing their validity. We have striven to show the rationale of objective-test construction, but ultimately it depends upon the concept of personality as the totality of behaviour, and the consequence of this that all individual differences must reflect personality differences. Also, since by definition objective tests are not face-valid, it is always necessary to demonstrate their validity. The main published battery of objective tests, the Objective Analytic Battery (Cattell and Schuerger, 1978), measures what are claimed to be the ten clearest objective T factors, but examination of the handbook to the test shows very little evidence for validity. This test desperately requires research. Indeed, all the emerging objective-test factors lack clear criterion-related evidence of validity. All that is known about the factors is their factor loadings on objective tests, but these, of course, are themselves of unknown validity. Thus the T factors discussed by Cattell are only speculatively identified. Given the present state of knowledge, it would be unwise to use these factors as bases for either theoretical or applied psychology.

This, however, is not to write off objective testing. It is indubitably promising, and with adequate research, objective-test factors could be identified and might prove valuable, especially in applied psychology.

We shall now describe briefly the few published objective tests. The somewhat speculative list of objective-test factors which have emerged from the tests will be examined in Chapter 7.

Published objective tests

The Objective Analytic Battery (OAB) (Cattell and Schuerger, 1978)

T (objective) factors in Cattell's system have a universal index number, which, it is hoped, will prove useful for fitting newly emerging factors into the system. This is the number which is set beside each variable of the OAB. In addition, it makes reference to factors in research particularly easy. The OAB is a group test, and a high school version has also been developed. OAB factors are listed below.

U.1.16. Ego standards or competitiveness Similar to factor C of the 16PF questionnaire (see p. 52) but more concerned with assertion.

U.1.19. Independence v. subduedness Similar to the second-order questionnaire factor of that name. This factor is related to the field independence of Witkin (1962).

U.1.20. Evasiveness A mixture of 'dubiousness of character, a tendency to posture toward the immediate group style and some emotional instability', exemplified by Mr Micawber (according to Cattell and Schuerger, 1978).

U.1.21. Exuberance Fluency, imagination and a fast natural tempo characterize this factor.

U.1.23. Capacity to mobilize v. regression Involving competence, flexibility and resistance to stress: a factor related to anxiety or neuroticism.

U.1.24. Anxiety This is the objective test counterpart of the second-order questionnaire anxiety factor which, together with extraversion, is regarded as the major personality factor.

U.1.25. Realism This is the P (psychoticism) factor of Eysenck.

U.1.28 Self-assurance

U.1.32. Exvia The objective-test factor corresponding to extraversion or exvia in questionnaires.

U.1.33. Discouragement v. sanguineness A factor of negative pessimism and hopelessness.

Objective tests used to measure the factors

The total testing time is just under four and a half hours, due to the very large number of tests used. We shall not list them all but shall sample a few tests from the battery. Usually the title is self-explanatory.

Modernistic drawings	(U.1.16) Subjects have to discover shapes in them
Rapid calculations	(U.1.16) Very simple sums
Picture memory	(U.1.19)
Opinions	(U.1.20) Subjects have to agree or disagree with statements
Human nature	(U.1.20) Subjects have to agree or disagree with statements about human nature
Writing speed	(U.1.23)
Comparing letters	(U.1.23) A test of accuracy
Humour test	(U.1.24) Jokes are rated for comic quality

So much for the OAB. As yet there is no firm evidence for validity, but clearly it is a personality test well deserving of research and one whose ingenuity is a credit to the originality of its author.

Two earlier objective tests developed by Cattell and his colleagues deserve mention, although the evidence for their validity is not strong. These are the Humour Test (Cattell and Luborsky, 1952), which requires subjects to rate preference for jokes and from which a number of factors are extracted. The Music Preference Test (Cattell and Eber, 1954) requires choices between pieces of music to be made, and again personality measures are scored from it.

Conclusions

The attempts to provide principles of objective-test construction depend ultimately upon the definition of personality as the sum total of behaviour – which means that any task which produces individual differences in performance is an objective test, given certain restraints on scoring – and upon how easy it is to guess what the test is measuring. Consequently, it is imperative that objective tests, if they are to be used other than in experimental investigations of their own validity (used, that is, as substantive measuring instruments), have clear, unequivocal demonstrations of validity. Unfortunately, in our view this has not been done. Cattell and Warburton (1965) are quite frank about the speculative identification of T factors in respect of most of the tests in their compendium and of most of the factors. Cattell and Schuerger (1978) write with greater certainty in the handbook to the OAB, but there is little convincing evidence. This, indeed, is the major problem with objective personality tests. What is now required is extensive research into their validity. Until this is done their use should be restricted to experimental research.

Summary

1 Objective tests were defined and two classification schemes were described as aids to an understanding of the rationale of their construction.
2 A number of objective tests were described and their constructive basis was discussed.
3 The advantages of objective tests were discussed, especially their resistance to faking and distortion.
4 The problem of establishing their validity was examined.
5 The main published objective test of personality, the Objective Analytic Battery, was described and discussed.
6 It was concluded that as yet objective tests are not ready for substantive use.

6 Measures of personality dynamics, moods and states

Defining our terms

The distinction between temperamental and dynamic traits

The personality questionnaires and objective tests that we have so far considered are concerned in the main with the temperamental aspects of personality, although projective tests are often designed to measure, *inter alia*, dynamic traits. According to the psychometric definition, temperament is conceived of in terms of traits that explain our ways of doing things. Many housewives wash up, but their methods are diverse in the extreme. Obsessionals meticulously clean and rinse the prongs of every fork and sterilize with disinfectants. Hysterics wash up with great speed, so that water is sprayed everywhere, breakages are common and the end result may be little cleaner than before.

Personality dynamics are concerned with the reasons for behaviour, basically with drives. The problem that the psychometrics of human dynamics broadly faces is the number and nature of these drives.

It can hardly be doubted that this is an important topic when we come to consider how different are the answers given to this question in clinical psychology. McDougall (1932) had a list of propensities and sentiments which included more than twenty propensities (e.g. food seeking, protection) and a far longer list of sentiments. Murray (1938) proposed an even longer list of needs, with their corresponding environmental presses. Freud (e.g. 1920) claimed that two drives could account for human dynamics – Eros and Thanatos. With the theories of clinicians even of this great eminence so much at odds, one conclusion is to be drawn: firm evidence must be provided, and it is with this evidence that the psychometrics of human dynamics is concerned. The tests to be examined in this chapter, therefore, will be those of dynamic traits or drives.

The fluctuation of dynamic traits   One aspect of the measurement of dynamic traits that must be constantly borne in mind is that they, or at least some of them, fluctuate over time. If we assume that there is a food-seeking drive, for example, it is obvious that this will vary in strength depending upon the time and size of the last meal, general health and what the future plans of the subject are. Thus a boxer may be hungry but may miss a meal just before a fight. Clearly, if we measure a subject's drive for food just after finishing an enormous meal, his hunger drive will be low. This has to be mentioned because it may be the case that conventional test–retest reliability coefficients are unsuited to tests of dynamic traits.

Moods and states

This discussion of the temporal instability of drives, depending in some cases upon degree of satiation or deprivation, leads us on to measures of moods and states, which we shall also examine in this chapter, both categories of variable which *prima facie* would appear likely to be related to drives and may even act as drives. Thus an angry (mood) husband may abuse his wife, which usually he does not do. Similarly, a man highly anxious (state) over the health of his daughter may drive with less attention than usual and scrape his car or forget a business appointment. On such an *a priori* intuitive analysis, therefore, it would appear likely that moods and states can also determine behaviour.

In the discussion above the terms 'moods' and 'state' were used. However, for the purposes of psychological measurement there seems to be no useful distinction. Indeed, as we have previously argued (Kline, 1979), the distinction appears to be one of idiom. Feelings such as boredom, energy, elation, frustration, bitterness are usually described as moods in common English usage, whereas anxiety is not often thought of in that way. In intuitive and clinical psychology the element common to states and moods is that they fluctuate over time and are often regarded as causes of behaviour. For the sake of simplicity, we shall subsume both moods and states under the term 'state'. For the sake of English style, we shall refer in discussion to moods or states where appropriate, but no conceptual distinction is intended.

The distinction between states and traits

Whereas the distinction between states and moods was regarded simply as one of English idiom, the difference between states and traits is considered to be of considerable psychological importance and is one that cannot be minimized. This distinction is best exemplified by anxiety, since state anxiety, at least, has been experienced by all but the most fortunate and is simply a part of everyday life experience.

State anxiety is caused by some particular event: a severe operation in the offing, a visit to the dentist, an impending examination, a visit to a prospective mother-in-law. All these, in our society, are common experiences, giving rise to state anxiety in all but the toughest.

Trait anxiety is the general anxiety level of an individual when nothing traumatic has happened or is about to happen. Trait anxiety, in fact, is measured by factor N of Eysenck, the anxiety factor of Cattell (both variables are discussed in Chapter 3), as well as by a number of other more specialized tests. At any given time the actual anxiety level of an individual is composed of state and trait anxiety. Were it possible to measure these components separately, state anxiety could be expected to fluctuate over time, while trait anxiety would probably not vary. There is an interaction between state and trait anxiety; the stolid, low-anxiety individual reacts little to events that make the highly trait-anxious subject almost panic-stricken.

This distinction between trait and state anxiety exemplifies the general distinction between the two categories of variable. Traits are relatively stable over time; states show considerable fluctuation.

This introductory discussion demonstrates that the psychometric study of motivation or personality dynamics must seek to measure (a) states, since these, however transitory, do appear to exert influence over behaviour; (b) basic human drives, with the aim of elucidating their number and nature.

Moods and states

We shall begin by examining the special measurement problems associated with states. As we have indicated, states are expected to fluctuate over time. Indeed, it is this lability that distinguishes them from traits. The first obvious difficulty, which is relatively trivial and can be overcome but must nevertheless be mentioned, concerns test–retest reliability and studies of validity.

Test–retest reliability

Whereas accurate trait measurement, by definition, implies high test–retest reliability, accurate state measurement, also by definition, should not be highly reliable over time. This means that conventional retest reliabilities should not be computed for tests of states. For these tests the critical coefficient of reliability is one of the measures of test homogeneity, preferably the alpha coefficient (see Chapter 1).

Validity

For measures of states predictive validity studies with a long time interval are generally not appropriate. Investigations of validity for state tests have to be designed basically using variations in state level that have been experimentally or naturally induced. Some examples will clarify this point.

State anxiety This could be measured in examination candidates, interviewees, those waiting in a dentist's waiting room. These subjects could be retested three weeks later, and we would expect the second set of scores to be significantly lower. These studies are, of course, examples of naturally induced variation. Obviously, there are ethical problems associated with inducing anxiety experimentally, and the present writer would not be prepared to do this. However, a relatively innocuous procedure that is often used with students consists of giving them difficult intelligence-test items which they fail, and then informing them that these items do measure ability. State anxiety test scores taken after such failure should be high.

State depression The ethical problems raised by the induction of experimental depression are such that it has rarely been attempted. Even the natural experiment produces ethical difficulties, since reactive depression is usually induced by particularly unpleasant traumata (e.g. deaths of spouses, parents or children; loss of job, house or a considerable amount of money; divorce or unwanted pregnancy). To expect subjects to fill in questionnaires at such a time, even *causa scientiae*, requires a certain determination. In principle, however, validity studies of a depression scale are perfectly possible.

As can be seen from these two examples, validity studies of mood scales can be undertaken: essentially, we make use of the fluctuations by relating them to external environmental events.

The correct form of analysis for state tests

This is a problem which is raised mainly by Cattell and his colleagues (e.g. Cattell and Kline, 1977; Kline, 1979), although the argument seems powerful. Cattell claims that any statistical method which is going to distinguish moods from traits must involve time, since the essential difference between them is that the trait is stable, while the state fluctuates over time. This means that there must be retesting. Now, the standard (R) factor analysis factors the correlations between tests taken at one time, searching for dimensions. Such R factors could be states; they could equally well be traits. Further studies would have to be carried out on such putative R state factors to ensure that they did fluctuate as hypothesized. Strictly, therefore, what is needed for the extraction of state factors is a factor analysis which includes retesting. There are three possible procedures.

P analysis   P analysis subjects to factor analysis the correlations between occasions on a number of variables for each individual separately. The emerging factors, therefore, are to be thought of as the dimensions accounting for the changes in scores between occasions, so according to our definition, these are states. P-factor analysis, therefore, must reveal within an individual the most important states over the period of testing.

Unfortunately, there are many practical difficulties that render P analyses less useful than their powerful logic suggests, and in fact there are few such studies in the research literature. The main difficulty lies in recruiting enough subjects who are willing to be retested many times over a considerable period of time. Even if a large enough sample can be collected, the psychological nature of such subjects, true gluttons for punishment, must be special in that they have volunteered: strictly, this makes proper psychological generalization difficult. In addition to this there is the technical psychometric problem of whether scores on repeated retesting are truly equivalent to each other, since tests are validated usually on first or second performance by subjects. If parallel forms are used, then there is the added uncertainty that is created by lack of perfect equivalence between the parallel forms.

All these practical problems have led Cattell to utilize methods that, if less elegant, involve less of the subjects' time.

dR technique   This involves an R analysis (of correlations between variables) of the *changes* in scores between two occasions. Emerging factors must account for the changes, and if they have been tested on stable traits, such factors should be states. This method involves only two testing sessions; thus large and representative samples can be utilized. Unfortunately, there is one difficulty which some psychometrists of good repute (e.g. Cronbach, 1970) regard as so important as to infirm the procedure. This is the unreliability of change scores. Cronbach (1970) argues that this is so great that further analysis, especially factor analysis, is too error-prone to be useful.

Chain P technique   This is a procedure which combines what is best in P analysis and dR factoring. As described by Cattell (1973), it consists of testing a group of subjects on a number of occasions – say five subjects on five occasions – and putting the results into a series (twenty-five occasions). Although this method overcomes the weakness of the dR method, which is that only two occasions are sampled, it clearly cannot be as powerful as P technique conducted on a large number of subjects.

Finally, a difficulty common to all methods must be mentioned. This concerns the intervals between retesting. It is obvious that short-term moods and states would not be observed by testing every day or once a week. Such volatile states can be investigated only by intensive study of individual cases, where such constant testing might be possible.

Despite these claims by Cattell and colleagues, which are certainly points well taken, most researchers into moods and states have been content to use R analysis in their investigation. Thus the mere emergence of factors is no guarantee that they are in fact state factors. However, the justification of this methodology rests on two arguments, of which only one is usually invoked.

The first argument is one of fact validity. The majority of mood scales have instructions asking the subjects to complete the items in accord with how they feel at the time of taking the test. If, therefore, the items behave as they appear (i.e. they are face-valid), the factors should reflect moods or states. The second argument involves real validity. Even if it is the case that the emerging factors could be trait factors, if evidence is adduced which demonstrates that they fluctuate with environmental events, as predicted if they were states, then the fact that they *could be* traits (which are by definition stable) is not relevant.

Consequently, although mood scales should be produced by P technique in an ideal world, R analysis can be used to produce mood and state measures provided that there is some real evidence for their validity. We shall now consider some of the more widely used mood scales.

Mood scales

The brief summary which is to follow owes much to an extensive survey of such tests which has been recently carried out by Howarth and Schockman-Gates (1980), a very useful and not entirely uncritical compilation which concentrates upon multiple mood scales, ignoring projective tests and measures of state anxiety.

The first point made by these authors is that whereas the leading trait measures described and discussed in earlier chapters are extensively used (as measured by the citations in Buros, 1978), mood scales are not much employed. However, the reasons for this are clear, since Howarth and Schockman-Gates are able to cite little evidence in support of the scales which they discuss, scales which are themselves selected as being among the best available. We shall not here mention those scales which are deemed of little validity but shall concentrate, as was the case with trait inventories, on those that seem capable of yielding substantive psychological findings.

The Nowlis Mood Adjective Checklist (Nowlis and Nowlis, 1956) consists of 140 adjectives which give rise to twelve mood factors, although in many studies not all adjectives are used. As Howarth and Schockman-Gates point out, it has formed the basis of many other mood tests. This list has been subjected to factor analysis, and twelve factors do seem to account for the variance: aggression, anxiety, surgery, elation, concentration, fatigue, social affection, sadness, scepticism, egotism, rigour and nonchalance.

Plutchik's Emotion-Mood Index, the Mood Profile Index and the Plutchik Affect Measure are all unpublished but are described by Howarth and Schockman-Gates. One scale published by Plutchik (1966) consists of eight terms to be rated on five-point scales. Plutchik argues that emotions and moods cannot be disentangled, and his scales are: fearful, angry, sad, surprised, expectant, joyful, disgusted and agreeable.

The Clyde Mood Scale (Clyde, 1960, 1963) is a check list of forty-eight adjectives claiming to measure six states – friendly, aggressive, clear-thinking, sleepy, unhappy and dizzy. The last three scales strongly suggest that it is not suitable for use with normal subjects in normal conditions, and indeed the test was designed for drug studies. This, as Lykken (1972) has argued, is a severe limitation of the scale.

Most of the other scales referred to by Howarth and Schockman-Gates are highly specialized, designed for work with psychotic patients and for drug studies, so that they are only marginally useful to general psychology. Since, in addition, there is little sound evidence for their validity, we shall not discuss them here.

None of the scales which we have described, although apparently the best of their kind, has clear evidence for validity, so that they should not be used even cautiously for the substantive psychological investigation of moods. Since, too, their method of construction (using R analysis) is dubious, we intend to say no more about them. We have included them simply so that readers can see the traditional approach to mood measurement. Clearly, what are needed are scales developed through P, dR or chain P technique, a conclusion with which Howarth and Schockman-Gates are in general agreement.

The Eight-State Questionnaire (Curran and Cattell, 1974) is a research questionnaire which claims to measure eight states: anxiety, stress, depression, regression, fatigue, guilt, extraversion and arousal. The only evidence for its validity rests on the notion of true factor validity, which is determined by the average factor loadings of items divided by the correlation between items, which is really a measure of the extent to which the items measure some factors, regardless of what those factors are. However, the basis of the construction of this test, according to Cattell (1973), was dR and chain P technique. As such it deserves scrutiny, although any findings would have to be interpreted with the utmost caution. This is a test which must be subjected to further research, and its factors should be validated.

These are the most important measures of states and moods; as can be seen, none of them can be regarded as a well validated test. It is this basic deficiency which accounts for the fact, noted by Howarth and Schockman-Gates (1980), that such tests are not widely used.

Before leaving these tests, mention should be made of one measure of state anxiety that does seem generally to be accepted as useful (see Buros, 1978, for example), that of Spielberger *et al.* (1970), the State–Trait Anxiety Inventory. Although based on R analysis, there is considerable research to suggest that the state factors are valid and do fluctuate in accordance with prediction (Katkin, 1978).

Finally, in our discussion of moods states and their tests a small distinction should perhaps be made. As Cattell (1973) and Cattell and Kline (1977) have argued, dR studies of traits and states reveal not only states, as measured by the Eight-State Questionnaire, but also trait-change factors (that is, fluctuating factors reflecting decline and growth in traits) rather than motivational states as such. However, little can be said of these, for little information is available. Readers should be aware of their existence. Enough has been said about moods and states, and we shall turn to the measurement of drives.

The measurement of drives

As we argued at the beginning of this chapter, the main question in respect of drives concerns their number and nature. As with the study of temperament and abilities, the psychometric approach is to measure the appropriate behaviour, driven behaviour, and to subject it to factor analysis. Obviously, to map out what might be called the 'motivational sphere', as many drives as possible must be sampled. In fact, this is the method pursued by Cattell and his colleagues (in work summarized by Cattell and Child, 1975; Cattell and Kline, 1977). Other researchers in this field have pursued a simplified procedure which we shall discuss briefly at the end of this chapter.

The work of Cattell

Cattell, in his efforts to define the motivational sphere, which is, of course, necessary before it can be sampled, adopts the viewpoint of McDougall in conceiving of drives as having three components: the tendency to attend to some stimuli rather than others; the accompanying emotion; the impulse as a cause of action. Given this concept of drive, it follows that a study of attitudes must reveal the structure of drives because attitude strength reflects the strength of an impulse to act in response to a stimulus.

The study of human dynamics summarized in Cattell and Child (1975) is far less well developed than that of temperament. The factors are more tentatively identified, and there is no large body of research indicating that they are very useful for predicting job success or in clinical diagnosis and treatment. Consequently, our discussion of these factors must be brief. In fact, the factor analysis of human dynamics has yielded two distinct sets of factors, one concerned with strength of interests and one concerned with the number and nature of the drives themselves.

Attitude strength Objective tests of attitudes or motivated behaviours were used. These were based on the claims made in mainly clinical psychology as to what constituted such driven behaviour. Cattell and Child (1975) list sixty-eight indices, which include physiological measures and such variables as a high level of information, perceptual skill, better memory for preferred material and less distraction. For example, the keen motorist will know huge lists of specifications and performances for cars, will be able to spot different makes at a distance and, when presented with material about cars, will remember it better than someone who is not interested in cars. The car bore is a well-known modern (mostly male) phenomenon. The results of factoring such tests have yielded five clear, first-order, strength-of-attitude factors and two second-orders:

1 alpha – conscious id: the 'I desire' component of attitudes;
2 beta – realized, integrated, rational interests;
3 gamma – the moral component of interests, the feeling that one ought to be interested in a subject.

These three factors are not unlike the ego, id and super-ego of psychoanalytic theory.

4 delta – the physiological factor: the tingling in the spine, the thrill at hearing an orchestra tune, prologue of delights to come;
5 epsilon – a factor relating to conflict;
6 and 7 zeta and theta – not yet identified: oblique factors.

At the second order two factors emerge:

1 the integrated component – loading on beta and gamma, reflecting reality-based experience;
2 the unintegrated component – loading on alpha, delta and epsilon, reflecting mainly the aspects of interest in strength below the level of awareness.

The meaning of these factors for the understanding of attitude strength is clear. Attitude strength will vary according to our position on these components. Thus measures of interest or attitude using a single score are unlikely to be valid – the reason why we have consigned our discussion of standard interest inventories to a brief final section. The psychological implications of these factors will be discussed in later chapters. At present there is no published test of these primary strength-of-attitude factors, although the integrated and unintegrated components can be measured by the Motivational Analysis Test (MAT) (Cattell *et al.*, 1970b), which we discuss below (see p. 89).

Dynamic structure factors In the work of Cattell these have emerged from the factor analysis of interests as measured by objective T tests which we have fully described in Chapter 5. The factors which we set out are those that are most commonly found in the research and are regarded as the most reliably identified by Cattell and Child (1975), in their account of the complex work on motivation, and by Cattell and Kline (1977), in their account of the whole corpus of Cattell's research into personality.

Before listing the factors, two of Cattell's neologisms must be defined – ergs and sentiments. An erg is 'an innate reactive tendency, the behaviours of which are directed towards and cease at a particular consummatory goal activity'. An erg, therefore, resembles a basic drive, the kind of variable that ought to be observable in mammalian species. In addition, however, rather different drives have been factor analytically identified. These are sentiments defined by Cattell and Child (1975) as 'dynamic structures visible as reaction patterns common to persons, objects or social institutions and upon which all people seem to have some degree of endowment'. The main ergs are food seeking, mating, narcissism (love of comfort and warmth), gregariousness, parental pity, exploration, fear, self-assertion, pugnacity and acquisitiveness. Important sentiments (at least in the West, for sentiments are essentially culturally acquired drives) are career, self-sentiment, parental family, super-ego, wife or sweetheart and religion. In addition, the factor analysis of interests has revealed factors which are of less interest but correspond to hobbies (e.g. sport) and scientific, business and aesthetic interests.

The importance of these results in understanding the dynamics of human behaviour is that the main ergs and sentiments must be regarded as the most important variables. This list of ergs shows that Murray (1938) and McDougall (1932) postulated too many human drives and Freud, on the other hand, too few.

Perusal of Cattell and Child (1975) makes it clear that these ergs and sentiments are not as powerfully supported by research as are the temperamental factors of personality. They are, at present, hypotheses rather than facts. However, there is little doubt that this factor-analytic approach using objective tests deserves further research. At present it is promising. Its potential requires development.

The Motivation Analysis Test (MAT) (Cattell et al., 1970b)

This is a published set of pencil-and-paper objective tests for measuring five ergs and sentiments – sex, assertion, fear, narcissm and pugnacity, together with self-sentiment, career, sweetheart–spouse, home–parental and super-ego sentiments. Integrated and unintegrated strength-of-attitude components are also measured by this test, for which high school and junior school versions exist.

If shown to be valid, the MAT could form a useful basis for exploring the implications of Cattell's work on personality dynamics. There are few studies of the validity of the MAT, although the present writer has carried out an interesting investigation of the test using P technique (Kline and Grindley, 1974), in which one subject was tested every day for twenty-eight days, and the changes in scores were then related to a diary kept daily over the same period. There were some convincing relationships. For example, the career sentiment was low and consistent over the period except for one day – that on which the subject went for an interview for a course in teacher training.

Further evidence of validity cited by Cattell and Child (1975) shows that manipulation of the hunger and sex drives in subjects does produce changes in the relevant MAT score (hunger is measured by a separate set of tests). Generally, therefore, there is some evidence supporting the use of the MAT, but it is strictly an experimental test. Cooper and Kline (1981) have carried out a factor and item analysis of the MAT, and it appears that some of the items do not fall into their appropriate scales, at least with our British sample.

Other approaches to the measurement of motivation

As we have argued, the emergence of a number of dimensions of interest strength and of a number of basic dynamic factors rather suggests that other approaches will not prove adequate. However, over the years psychometrics – catering for the demands of industrial psychology, which requires tests of motivation for selection and guidance procedures – has developed tests of interests. The notion of interests which they have used is the simple, everyday one based upon intuition and common sense, and most of these tests have been developed by criterion keying (i.e. items have been included in scales if they discriminate holders of the relevant job from others). Another method of motivation-test construction has been to try to write items fitting Murray's (1938) description of needs and presses and then to select the items by means of the usual test-construction methods (see Chapter 3). Among the best-known of such tests are the following.

Criterion-keyed tests   such as the Strong Interest Blank (Strong *et al.*, 1971), which measures twenty-two interest scales, and the Kuder Preference Tests (Kuder, 1970), which measure a smaller number of broader interests, such as outdoor activities, mechanical skills and an interest in people. As we have argued in detail elsewhere (Kline, 1975), these tests can be said to be positively baleful in their influence in applied psychology because even if they do discriminate between groups, they offer no psychological insights into the reasons for such discrimination by virtue of their construction. They cannot contribute to substantive psychological knowledge. They measure how similar subjects are to criterion groups in terms of responses to sets of items.

Tests constructed to fit Murray's theory of needs and presses   such as the Edwards Personal Preference Schedule (EPPS) (Edwards, 1959) and Jackson's Personality Research Form (Jackson, 1974). These tests, although carefully constructed – indeed, the Jackson test is in some respects a model of careful test construction (Anastasi, 1972) – suffer from two defects. There is little independent evidence that Murray's personological theory is, in fact, a useful way to encapsulate human personality, and indeed the factor-analytic evidence strongly suggests that it is not. Thus, as a basis for test construction it is not satisfactory.

Furthermore, there is little evidence for the validity of either of these tests. The EPPS, although widely used (more than 1000 references up to 1972; see Buros, 1972), is simply assumed to be valid by its users, and in any case it was constructed by Edwards as an exercise in test construction (the minimization of social desirability response set). The Jackson test, on the other hand, offers some evidence of validity, but this is only ratings by self and peers. This is unsatisfactory, and until the construct and predictive validity of the test is demonstrated, it must be used only with extreme caution.

Conclusions concerning the psychometry of motivation

Generally, as can be seen, the study of dynamic structure is far less advanced than was the case with temperament. The only workers in this field with a broad factor-analytic approach are Cattell and his colleagues, and their work is still largely improven, although of great promise. The standard psychometric approach does not seem likely to be highly useful in yielding substantive psychological findings, however valuable it may be in practice. Clearly, in this field a huge research task awaits.

Summary

1 The distinction between dynamic and temperamental personality traits was drawn.
2 Moods and states were differentiated from drives.
3 The distinction between traits and states was made.
4 Problems with the measurement of moods and states were described.
5 The correct form of analysis for states was outlined.
6 Some mood scales were described and evaluated.
7 Cattell's work on the measurement of drives was described.
8 Strength-of-attitude factors were listed.
9 Dynamic structure factors were listed, and the MAT was described.
10 Other approaches to interest measurement and their resulting tests were described.

7 The empirical basis for a theory of personality

A perusal of modern textbooks on personality (e.g. Pervin, 1975; Hall and Lindzey, 1955, and its later editions) makes it clear that a strong scientific objection to many theories of personality can be made on account of the data on which they are based. The scientific method generally demands that observations should be reliable, and quantification is essential. Even given these simple criteria, psychoanalytic theories are wanting. Thus the data of Freudian theory are reputedly the free associations of patients. However, these are rarely given. Instead we find a brilliant series of interpretations of such material. Similar objections can be raised to all brands of psychoanalytic theory. McDougall (1932) speculates about human nature, citing a variety of evidence, none of which is quantified or precisely quoted. Murray's personology (1938) has a basis of data. These, however, are essays, projective-test protocols and interviews, all subject to interpretative fancies and far from the precise, replicable, quantified scores that are required. This is not to write off these theories as worthless, as Eysenck (1957b) has done, for they indubitably contain powerful insights into the psychology of personality which can indeed (and should) be placed on a more scientific basis. Indeed, the present writer has attempted to do this with Freudian theory (Kline, 1972).

This lack and need of firm data for theorizing about personality is what makes the psychometric approach to personality so important. For we argue that the psychological tests of personality that we have reviewed in Chapters 3–6, especially those based on factor analysis, have, in fact, revealed some of the most important constructs in the field, and consequently their variables should be used as a basis for any theorizing in personality: that is to say that any personality theory should be consonant with the factors that have emerged from the psychometric analysis of personality.

In this chapter, therefore, we shall briefly set out and describe the factors that have been revealed by the most important personality tests. In subsequent chapters attempts to utilize them in theories will be examined.

The best-established temperamental factors

It would be pleasant to set out a list of temperamental factors that all (or even almost all) investigators agreed were the most well founded or important in the field of human temperament. This, alas, is not possible. As we saw from our description of factor analysis in Chapter 3, not only are there many possible solutions (although the notion of rotation to simple structure has eased this difficulty), but in addition there are various technical requirements for carrying out good factor analyses which are not always adequately met. A combination of all these circumstances has led to the unfortunate fact that each of several leading workers claims that his set of factors offers the best description of personality: Guilford (e.g. Guilford and Zimmerman, 1949), using orthogonal factors; Comrey (1970), using clusters of items, the FHIDs, as the basis of the correlational matrix; Eysenck (Eysenck and Eysenck, 1975), with his so-called super-factors; Howarth (Browne and Howarth, 1977), who has attempted a synthesis of many personality inventories; and finally Cattell (Cattell and Kline, 1977; Cattell, 1980), with a massive research background to his sixteen factors.

The answer to the question, could it even be answered in the present state of knowledge, is highly tendentious and depends to a large extent on complex technical problems with factoring methods and ultimately on subjective judgements concerning the adequacy of factorial solutions. Kline (1979), in *Psychometrics and Psychology*, attempted to draw up just such a list, justifying his selection of factors on technical grounds. However, recent research carried out by Kline and colleagues at Exeter has to some extent thrown those claims into confusion.

Our solution to this difficulty in a book of this type is to summarize our arguments and research findings concerning the various sets of factors without going too far into technical detail and allowing for the possibility that future research results may cause some of our conclusions to be changed. In some cases the arguments are central to the thesis of the book, and these will be discussed in later chapters as indicated. For greater detail readers are referred to Cattell and Kline (1977) and Kline (1979).

Despite these problems, almost all factorists seem agreed that two temperamental factors account for a large proportion of variance in personality questionnaires. These two factors have numerous correlations with external criteria, a further confirmation of their importance.

Extraversion

This is a dimension, introversion–extraversion, with the majority of the population at the mid-point, thus distinguishing it from the typology developed by Jung (1923). The extravert is sociable, gregarious, cheerful, talkative, lively and outgoing. The introvert, by contrast, is quiet, withdrawn, bookish and somewhat inhibited. This dimension has been linked by Eysenck (1967) to the arousability of the central nervous system and to conditionability, and hence to many aspects of social learning, thereby implicating personality in pathology, psychopathy and political beliefs, all of which are fully discussed in Chapter 9.

Extraversion, it will be remembered from Chapter 3, is in fact measured by most of the personality tests which we there examined. The most widely used measure is the EPQ (Eysenck and Eysenck, 1975) and its forerunner, the EPI (Eysenck and Eysenck, 1964). Extraversion can also be measured by Cattell's 16PF questionnaire (Cattell *et al.*, 1970a) where it appears as a second-order factor, called by him exvia, but agreed to be identical with extraversion (Cattell and Kline, 1977).

This raises a technical difficulty, which we shall have to examine in our Chapter 9 on the theories of Cattell and Eysenck but of which it is necessary to be aware in a study of the main personality factors. Eysenck prefers to take out a few important factors because he regards these as highly reliable and replicable, as indeed they are (Eysenck and Eysenck, 1969). Cattell (1973), however, considers that this approach loses information. He prefers to take out a large number of primary factors, as many as can be found in replicable simple-structure rotations, and to combine these to arrive at the broader secondary factors. Thus there is agreement with Eysenck that extraversion is an important factor, but Cattell argues that a knowledge of its constituent primary factors is also valuable. We agree with Cattell in principle, although, as we shall see in Chapter 9 and as we claim in this chapter, the nature of these primary factors is difficult to ascertain.

In research by Barrett and Kline (1980), in which the EPQ items were factored, Eysenck's factors appeared at the second order when a large number of primaries were extracted (as Cattell would expect), but when only four (N, E, P and L) were extracted and rotated, these appeared clearly at the first order. The one clear conclusion from this research is that extraversion is unquestionably a major personality factor.

Anxiety or neuroticism

This, again, is a factor which emerges from most factored personality tests, and there is little doubt that much of the variance in the MMPI, a criterion-keyed test, is accounted for by this factor (see Dahlstrom and Welsh, 1960, for example). As was the case with extraversion, this is directly measured by the EPQ and EPI and indirectly, at the second-order level, by the 16PF Test. Guilford's test also contains a measure (E), as does that of Comrey (S).

There is no dispute among any of these factorists that the same factor is being measured. However, there is disagreement (although not considerable) concerning its interpretation and hence its name. Eysenck considers this factor to be neuroticism because it is the underlying personality trait predisposing an individual to respond to stress with neurotic symptoms (Eysenck, 1967). Cattell, on the other hand (Cattell, 1973; Cattell and Kline, 1977), would not deny this point, but he argues that neurotics differ from normals on other factors in addition; hence the label 'neuroticism' is misleading, and he prefers the term 'anxiety'. Since this latter seems to embrace the notion of neuroticism, it seems preferable to us. This again will be fully discussed in Chapter 9.

Anxiety is a dimension with the majority of the population at the mid-point. The highly stable individual obtains a low score on anxiety (i.e. below the mean), but the psychological significance of the extreme low-scorer is not clear. The typical high-scoring, anxious subject worries a lot, tends to feel depressed, has rather considerable mood swings, sweats easily, feels sick before important events and, indeed, fits generally the everyday concept of an anxious individual. Eysenck (1967) links this dimension to the lability of the autonomic nervous system and this, if true, would account for the well-known physical concomitants of anxiety.

Barrett and Kline, in the research referred to above, found that, as was the case with extraversion, N emerged with perfect clarity (all N items loading high on the factor) at both the first order and the second order.

There is no doubt that in the temperamental field E and N are two dimensions which are fundamental aspects of personality. If only two personality variables could be measured in any investigation, these would be the two to choose, unless, of course, some specific hypothesis that clearly demanded the measurement of some other factor were being investigated.

Psychoticism

Originally, Eysenck's personality theory (e.g. Eysenck, 1947) was a two-factor theory, claiming that much of personality could be understood in terms of two orthogonal factors, extraversion and neuroticism. Recently, a third factor has been added, P (psychoticism), which is measured by the EPQ, this being the test's main feature that differentiates it from the EPI. Eysenck and Eysenck (1976), in their book on psychoticism, admit that less is known about this factor than about E or N. Before the EPQ it had been measured by objective tests such as vigilance tasks and variability in reaction times (Eysenck and Eysenck, 1968) but until the advent of the EPQ had proved difficult to capture using personality test items.

The high scorer is solitary, does not care for people, is troublesome, does not fit in, is hostile, cold and aggressive even to his family. He likes the bizarre and the strange and enjoys upsetting and making a fool of people. Perhaps the key to the high psychoticism scorer is lack of empathy. This factor distinguishes psychotics (schizophrenics, paranoids, for example) from neurotics and normals.

A few points need to be made about psychoticism. First, it is, again, a dimension. However, it differs from E and N in that the majority of the population score low on this test. This uneven split in a normal sample of item responses may be responsible for the finding by Barrett and Kline (1980) that P was not as robust factorially as the other two scales. A good spread on this scale may usually be obtained by using samples combined of normals and abnormals. The underlying physiology of P is not confidently asserted by the Eysencks (1976), although it is possibly related to the androgen level of the blood.

We shall not discuss P further here, since its psychological significance is more fully discussed in Chapter 11 on applied psychology and in Chapter 9. It seems a factor worthy of inclusion, as it is clearly a component of personality implicated in psychosis, a condition not well understood in terms of personality variables. Most other personality tests designed for normals do not contain a measure of psychoticism, and in Cattell's system the nearest approach to it is to be found in the abnormal factors which do not appear in the 16PF. However, some of these could be identified with P, which may be effectively a second-order abnormal factor.

Although there is argument about whether N, E and P are secondary or primary factors, there is no question that they do appear at the second order and even at higher orders (as in Eysenck and Eysenck, 1969), so that it makes sense to think of them as higher-order factors. In conclusion, therefore, we claim that any adequate theory of personality must subsume these three higher-order personality factors.

Before examining any primary factors that ought to be woven into personality theories, we must consider briefly whether any other higher-order factors deserve inclusion, even though they may not be as pervasive as the three discussed above.

Higher-order analysis of the Cattell primary factors (Cattell *et al.*, 1970a; Cattell, 1973; Cattell and Kline, 1977) usually reveals four clear second orders: exvia and anxiety, which we have discussed, and two further factors, cortertia and independence.

Cortertia

This dreadful neologism is supposed to indicate this factor's interpretation as cortical alertness. The low-scoring subject is warm and sentimental, a lover of the arts. The high-scoring subject is alert, realistic, practical: his feelings are well controlled. This factor resembles a dimension of personality which was mooted as early as the 1890s by William James (1890) – tough- v. tender-mindedness. Eysenck (1954) utilizes this dimension in explicating political behaviour, Fascists and communists being alike on this dimension, as are all advocates of totalitarian regimes.

Independence

The independent person is assertive, unconventional, active and responsive, refusing to be tamed by experience. This, indeed, is a dimension which is familiar in everyday observation.

With less confidence than with N, E and P, it can be argued that these two factors should be included in any theory of personality that seeks to embrace quantified data. It is interesting to note that the work of French (e.g. French *et al.*, 1963), who over the years has surveyed factorial studies of personality and has attempted to verify the factors claimed to be found (work which ignores problems of factorial methodology and much of Cattell's results), essentially shows these same four factors, although it does not name them thus, as Brand (1980) points out.

We now come to the more difficult problem of the primary factors: which ones, if any, should be included in our theoretical accounts? The difficulty, as we saw from our description of the tests, is that there are a large number of sets which have surprisingly little in common. If all were included, any theoretical account would be uselessly cumbersome.

Despite their different names, it is likely *a priori* that sets of primary factors overlap to some extent, especially given that different factor-analytic techniques have been used to extract the factors. Kline (1979) has surveyed the critical studies in which these different factor sets have been rotated together. A number of conclusions about these sets can be drawn.

1 The Guilford factors are orthogonal; when rotated to oblique simple structure, they appear to take up positions close to the Cattell factors (Cattell and Gibbons, 1968). This means, essentially, that they are not different from the Cattell factors.

2 The Comrey set of factors suffer from poor rotations (Cattell, 1973), and in addition, by virtue of their construction where groups of items form the basis of correlation rather than individual items, they are likely to be second-order factors. In fact, Barton (1973) (quoted by Cattell, 1973) rotated these factors, together with those of Cattell, to simple structure and found this to be so. Essentially, then, the Comrey factors are roughly equivalent to the second-order factors which we have so far discussed.

3 The Cattell primary factors. There is a real problem with the Cattell factors. Eysenck and Eysenck (1969) factored chosen items from the scales and failed to find the sixteen primary factors. Cattell (1972) claimed that there were methodological flaws in this study and presented results from 780 subjects which showed the sixteen factors with reasonable clarity. Saville and Blinkhorn (1976) demonstrated that the scales were not homogeneous and that the parallel forms were far from parallel. This lack of homogeneity, which has been known since the study by Levonian

(1961) is, of course, thought by Cattell to add to, rather than distract from, validity. Browne and Howarth (1977), in their huge investigation of questionnaires, also failed to find the Cattell factors, but they altered the wording of the items; and Vagy and Hammond (1976), replicating Eysenck's study, again failed to find the Cattell factors. Barrett and Kline (1982) factored the Cattell items on 500 subjects. The sixteen factors did not emerge: at best nine factors were extracted, and these were composite measures. Simple structure was reached using Direct Oblimin, so it is difficult to impugn this study. The consensus of results with technically reasonable factor methods is clear. The Cattell factors do not seem sufficiently stable at the first order to be included in a basic set of dimensions for incorporation into a personality theory.

4 Other factors. In our chapter on personality questionnaires we described the Dynamic Personality Inventory (Grygier, 1961). In a study of the validity of this test, Kline and Storey (1978) factored it with the Cattell and Eysenck scales and a number of other psychosexual personality scales. One clear factor emerged which, in our view, should be included in any basic list of personality dimensions. This was the obsessional personality factor – evident in the neat, orderly, pedantic, clean, self-controlled and controlling individual who, often with a little moustache, is to be seen wielding petty tyranny in the lower echelons of bureaucracies. This factor was found by Kline (1968) in a previous study of the Dynamic Personality Inventory and can be individually measured by his own test, Ai3Q (Kline, 1971), which was specially designed for measuring the Freudian anal character (Freud, 1908), a closely related syndrome. Indeed, the obsessional personality is a well-known category in the psychiatric literature (Mayer-Goss *et al.*, 1967) and in phenomenological psychiatry where it named the anancastic psychopath (Schneider, 1958).

In the 1978 study two other factors emerged which were entirely independent of the Cattell and Eysenck scales and which, on grounds of everyday observation, make considerable psychological sense – masculine and feminine attitudes. Although such factors run counter to the egalitarian *Zeitgeist*, and we may suffer insult from female libertarians, the notions of masculinity and femininity are supported by studies of the behaviour of non-human organisms (Hinde, 1966). These factors should probably be embraced by theories of personality. It is interesting to note that both Guilford and Comrey have masculinity factors among their scales.

5 Finally, it is probable that such well-known constructs as the authoritarian personality (Adorno *et al.*, 1950), dogmatism (Rokeach, 1960) are variants of, and essentially similar to, the obsessional factor, so that there is no reason to think that our list of factors would fail to encapsulate these syndromes.

This completes our list of temperamental factors. This is not to argue that this is a final list or that there are no other factors. Rather, it is claimed that at present these are factors sufficiently well established, and accord with enough other sources of evidence, to make it important that any personality theory properly accounts for them.

Motivational factors

Here we are in far greater difficulties than was the case with temperamental factors in establishing anything remotely resembling a definitive list.

Studies of interests *per se*, although revealing factors, surely reflect little more than the known interests of individuals, which vary from culture to culture and are not of fundamental importance to a basic psychodynamic psychology. Hence they are not the kind of factors to be included in our list.

Personality tests based upon Murray's needs and presses, which have been developed by Edwards (1959) and more recently by Jackson (1974), are also of dubious worth, since despite the technical expertise in the construction of the scales, the evidence for the validity of these scales as measures of needs is slight (Hogan, 1978). Furthermore, factoring the PRF with the Cattell scales indicates a considerable overlap of test variance (Nesselroade and Boltes, 1975). In addition, there is little support for Murray's (1938) personological theories: indeed, it was a curious basis for the construction of a personality test.

Cattell and Child (1975) present a reasonable case for the MAT as a measure of ten basic ergs and sentiments. However, there is still no firm evidence for the validity of these scales, although the case study by Kline and Grindley (1974), in which factor scores were related to diary records, seemed to support it. However, Cooper and Kline (1980) have recently submitted the MAT to an item and factor analysis of the item intercorrelations. This was extremely disappointing, since the items failed to form scales, and this throws doubt on the validity of the test. It appears to us that this work on ergs and sentiments demands much more research before any of the factors in the dynamic sphere can be regarded as well established.

This means that at present there are no factors that are sufficiently clear and well replicated in the dynamic sphere to demand accountability by a theory. However, this does not mean that an adequate personality theory needs no dynamic factors. On the contrary, they are necessary. At present, howryne, the state of dynamic factor research is such that we cannot yet state with any confidence what the main factors are. Tentatively we might insert the ergs and sentiments *faute de mieux*, a point to be taken up in Chapter 8.

Mood and state factors

As we saw in Chapter 6, the mood and state factors are not yet well established. Briefly, the commonly used mood scales, such as the Nowlis and the Clyde scales, are rather simple measures which go little beyond common-sense observation and have no strong evidence for validity. Furthermore, their method of construction fails to ensure that they are dynamic rather than temperamental variables. Similarly, the Cattell eight-state battery, although constructed by P and dR technique, is not highly validated.

Without further research a definitive list of mood and state factors is risky, although such a list is a necessity for any adequate personality theory. Tentatively, the list suggested by Cattell in the eight-state battery might be used as a base, selecting out the best validated variables.

Amid this gloom of insufficient research, however, one state factor must be included. This, of course, is state anxiety, about which there is complete agreement. Howarth (1980), while arguing as we do, that mood scales other than the eight-state battery have been wrongly constructed, claims that the best of the mood scales are optimism, depression, anger, vigour, confusion, anxiety and social affection.

At present, then, the best that can be done is to choose mood factors on which Cattell and other writers agree. These would be anxiety and depression. However, this list is likely to be amended in the light of further research.

Such, then, are the factors which at present any adequate personality theory must take into account. The dynamic and state factors are only tentative.

The remainder of this book will examine how this can be and has been done. In addition, the use of these factors in applied psychology will be discussed.

Summary

1 The need for a firm data base for theories of personality was argued.
2 Factor analysis was shown to be a technique capable of yielding the fundamental variables for theorizing.
3 The best established factors in the field of temperament were set out and described: extraversion, anxiety, psychoticism, cortertia and independence.
4 Among primary factors, masculinity, femininity and obsessional character were claimed to be important.
5 Dynamic factors were not so confidently set out; the ergs and sentiments of the MAT were tentatively suggested as important factors.
6 Mood and state factors were then set out. Again, anxiety and depression were tentatively included in the list.
7 This list, it was argued, is not final. Future research must clarify the major factors in these fields.

8 A psychometric model of man: in defence of traits

In the first seven chapters of this book we have proposed the following argument. Factor analysis is a statistical method capable of picking out the most important dimensions accounting for the variance in our observations. Applied to personality in the form of questionnaires and objective tests of temperament, dynamics and states, a number of factors about which there is little disagreement emerged. These factors should form part of any scientific theory of personality.

In this chapter we shall set out a model of personality, a psychometric model, which is built around the findings which we have discussed. This model is a general model which in principle can accept any set of psychometric factor-analytic results. Since this model itself has certain implicit assumptions, these will be examined. Finally, the implications of this psychometric model, both theoretical and in applied psychology, will be discussed.

Outline of the model

The factor analysis of human psychological variables has generally revealed categories of factors which are relatively independent of each other and which can be labelled, on examination of their most salient variables, as abilities, temperamental traits, dynamic traits and states. This, of course, is the quintessence of Cattell's huge corpus of factor-analytic investigations (Cattell, 1980) and is a conclusion with which few factorists would disagree.

The psychometric model claims, as was argued in Kline (1980), that any given behaviour is a function of these four categories of factors and their interaction with the relevant stimulus situation. It is to be noted in respect to this model that, unlike many clinical theories of personality, it is easily testable. The various factors are measured, together with the situational stimuli and the criterion behaviour. With this last a multiple correlation is computed. If it is inadequate, this coefficient will be 0. The beta weights will indicate the relative importance of the variables in the equation. As more extensive research is undertaken into dynamic and state variables, for example, it is to be expected that the correlations will rise.

Notes concerning the model

Definition of the factorial categories

We have already assumed these distinctions in our earlier chapters, where temperament, motivation and state were somewhat intuitively discriminated. However, as Cattell and Warburton (1965) point out, a more rigorous definition is difficult. In this book we do not deal with abilities – and by these we refer to the problem-solving skills that are most commonly found in tests of intelligence and in the more specific skills involved in educational attainment (numerical, verbal and spatial ability, for example).

Indeed, in our view a simple, intuitive distinction between these categories is probably as good as any, remembering that statistically the categories are distinct and that the correlations within category members are greater than those between members of different categories. After all, few would wrongly classify spatial ability, rage, anxiety and sexual drive.

Choice of variables in the equations

The most important variables (i.e. those accounting for the most variance) within each category should be used in the model. That is why the model is so useful for the purposes of our book, which is to incorporate the main personality factors into a theoretical psychology. As we saw in the earlier chapters, in some of the categories the most important factors have still to be discovered. Hence any actual results achieved with the model are likely to be improved upon with further research.

In the temperamental field we can feel reasonably confident that the largest factors have been found. In the field of abilities there can be equal confidence. As the work of Hakstian and Cattell (1974) and Cattell (1971b) has shown, two factors alone, fluid and crystallized abilities, would do much to cover the variance, especially if we were attempting to predict real-life performance in occupations or education. Sometimes certain behaviours might require a particular specific variable (e.g. some special ability, as perhaps in dentistry) for accurate prediction. This would, of course, have to be included.

The basic equation of the model

The basic equation states that any act or behaviour of an individual can be predicted from the linear addition of his scores on the major factors of ability, temperament dynamics and states, together with some measures of the environmental stimulus, all weighted in accordance with their importance for the criterion behaviour.

The specification equation

$$a_{iJ} = b_{J1} \, F_{1i} + b_{J2} \, F_{2i} \ldots + b_{JN} \, F_{Ni}$$

Where a, the action in situation J for individual i, is best estimated by the status of i on factors F_1 to F_N and by the weights b_J on the factors for the situation.

Notes concerning the specification equation

The linearity and additivity of the model The specification equation is a simple linear equation. However, as Cattell (1973) has argued, until this simple model is shown to be false empirically there is little point in attempting to produce a more elaborate version. What results there are with this model (which we discuss in the relevant chapters) do not suggest that its simplicity renders it worthless. In fact, Cattell (1973) and Cattell and Child (1975) produce some highly elaborated versions of this model. These elaborations, which at the present stage of research are only speculative, are designed to take account of the integrative function of the dynamic factors, super-ego and self-sentiment, functions which are part of Cattell's dynamic theories and which will be fully discussed in Chapter 9. They also try to weave the situation into the equations by involving state liability traits. However, we shall not discuss these modifications here because they are not essential to the psychometric model. Rather, they have been carried out to make the model fit more closely a particular theory of personality (that of Cattell) which is only one possible theoretical account, an account which has been fully worked out in Cattell (1980) but which is far ahead of any research evidence.

The psychometric model and the situation It should go almost without saying that situations affect behaviour. Few would play Punk rock on their transistors in a huge cathedral or, conversely, attempt a philosophical sermon at a rock festival. The psychometric model can deal with the situation (although no research has yet been carried out to check these ideas). This is done by assuming that for each state (including moods) there is a state liability trait on which individuals vary, as they do on other traits. This liability trait is transformed by a modulator, which expresses the average stimulation of a given stimulus for a state. An example will clarify this notion. Let us take the sex erg. For males, a beautiful naked woman has a high average value; Mrs Thatcher in full spate has a low value; while stimuli such as a cricket match or an old oak tree have none. Thus what is necessary is to develop situational indices to modulate state liability traits. Unfortunately, this huge task of situational measurement has not begun, so that at present such modulations cannot be included in specification equations. For this reason our basic psychometric model does not show such indices.

In fact, the importance of the situation in understanding behaviour has been recently heavily emphasized, especially in the writings of Mischel (e.g. 1973). Indeed, the term 'situationalism' has been coined to describe this approach, which minimizes the influence of traits (and hence, implicitly, denies the force of the psychometric model). This we discuss later in this chapter, once the psychometric model has been properly explicated.

The weights in the model   The weights of the variables for specifying each behaviour are determined empirically, and are essentially the beta weights obtained in multiple regressions of the selected variables to the behaviour. This means, of course, that good sampling and cross-validating studies on new samples are necessary.

Testing the model   The test of the model, as we have indicated, is powerful and simple. If the model were perfect, totally without error, our correlations would be 1. The further they depart from 1 and approach zero, the worse the model. The few tests of the model that exist demonstrate that correlations of around 0.3 to 0.5 can be obtained. Whether this result be due to the problems of the model *per se* (e.g. its additivity or linearity), to the choice of variables, to inefficient measures, to problems of the criterion measure or to any or all of these is not yet clear. Of course, correlation between any given behaviour and any variable within the domains (i.e. ability, temperament, motivation and state) is patent support for the model, since a multiple correlation with the others would in all likelihood be higher, and almost certainly as high.

Limitations of the model   One clear limitation of the model is in the kind of behaviour it is reasonable to expect it to predict. In our view, this model should be expected to predict important aspects of behaviour, such as occupation, academic success, hobbies – behaviours dependent on the nature of the individual, stable, long-lasting behaviours. Our reasons for this can be found below. We would not expect it to predict with accuracy short-term specific behaviours of no importance to the individual – behaviours, indeed, that might well be situationally determined.

Implications of the model   If the model works to any extent at all, this is evidence of the importance of traits of all kinds in the prediction of human behaviour. This is, therefore, of crucial interest in the situationist–trait debate which we discuss below. Thus it can be seen that the psychometric model is really a variant of the trait model.

Of course, if a trait model works, the research implications are indubitable. The development and nature of these traits must be studied, for an understanding of these yields an understanding of behaviour. Thus the testing of this model has profound implications for the study and understanding of personality, as well as for applied psychology.

If, on the other hand, the psychometric model fails and no juggling with variables and specification equations produces results, then either trait psychology is worthless, or factor analysis cannot yield the fundamental variables of the fields wherein it is used, as we have argued, or alternatively both implications are correct.

Whether positive or negative in outcome, therefore, testing the psychometric model will produce useful psychological knowledge.

The psychometric model and situationalism

Since the publication of Mischel's (1968) book on personality, trait theories of personality of the kind proposed in the psychometric model have fallen into disfavour. Mischel's claim that behaviour is situationally determined rather than resulting from traits on which individuals differ suited the egalitarian *Zeitgeist*. Harré (1980), indeed, claimed that he did not believe in traits, implying, as a philosopher, that this was the general belief of psychologists.

Regrettably, this absurd dogma has a strong hold on the British psychological establishment, and research funds for trait studies of personality are not easily come by, which in part accounts for the dearth of crucial experimental evidence.

Mischel's approach has come to be known as 'situationalism', and it is necessary to examine these claims so that the psychometric model can be properly evaluated. Although this is a contentious debate with a large literature, the task of summarizing has been hugely eased by the publication of an excellent paper on this very point by Eysenck and Eysenck (1980), whose views (in this topic) are in close agreement with those argued throughout this book. Our summary here owes much to this paper.

Critics of the trait model claim, essentially, that it cannot be correct because consistency of behaviour is rarely observed. The work of Hartshorne and May (1928, 1929), who found that children cheated in some experimental situations but not in others (thus, in their view, casting doubt on the trait of honesty), is often cited as a study which shows behavioural inconsistency, although this is not necessarily so. One powerful argument against the experimental work of Hartshorne and May is that neither of the experiments was tapping honesty, since cheating in experimental tasks of this kind has only face validity as a test. Furthermore, the reliability of these tests was low, thus rendering any correlations low.

Eysenck and Eysenck (1980) have assembled twelve counter-arguments. We shall discuss here what seem to be the most important of these arguments. Mischel's (1977a) major claim that the consistency of measurement in personality is low, with correlations only rarely above 0.3, applies in the main to studies of objective test data, as Block (1977) pointed out. Ratings and questionnaires, in fact, showed consistency, and a study of the consistency of emotional experiences by Epstein (1977) showed reliabilities of around 0.80. Mischel (1977), in his most recent paper, has accepted that these kind of data can be consistent, but that traits have to be interpreted in the context of their interaction with the environment (i.e. the situation) – a view with which the psychometric model agrees.

However, despite this admission, Mischel (e.g. 1973) would still prefer not to consider traits. He argues that the notion of trait is a scientific naiveté. Thus if we see a person acting honestly, we say he is 'high on honesty' and explain the behaviour by a concept that was derived only from the observation of that behaviour. However, while logically impeccable, the argument is trivial if, in fact, traits can predict external behaviour – and they can.

Thus Eysenck (1971) has shown that extraversion is related to the following variables (we quote from Eysenck and Eysenck, 1980):

sensory threshold; pain threshold; time estimation; sensory deprivation; perceptual defence; vigilance; critical flicker fusion; sleep–wakefulness patterns; visual constancy; figural after-effects; visual masking; rest pauses in tapping; speech patterns; conditioning; reminiscence; and expressive behaviour.

In addition, examination of the technical handbook to the 16PF test (Cattell *et al.*, 1970a) indicates that a large variety of different occupational groups can be discriminated by the personality traits measured in this test – all of which would be impossible if behaviour were not consistent. Given the unreliability of these scales, some of these observed correlations are surprisingly high.

Indeed, in our view much of the situationalist argument is made pointless by the fact that trait measures do in fact correlate substantially with a variety of external criteria, educational, clinical and occupational.

At this point some readers may be impatient with this whole debate. After all, we know people are consistent. As we have argued before (Kline, 1979), dockers are not noted as aesthetes or ballet dancers, nor chess masters renowned as town criers or wrestlers. Such common-sense observation is rejected by Mischel (1968), and even by Vernon (1964), as merely 'halo effect' and the stereotyping of observers. Once we have decided what a person is like, we forget all behaviour that does not fit the picture and retain only what fits. However, again the evidence does not support this claim. Willet (1964), for example, found that dangerous drivers (as convicted in the courts) were highly likely to have been convicted of other serious crimes. Thus the lunatic driver is a criminal, careless of life.

A final argument produced by the situationalists is that even if ratings of subjects do have a replicable factorial structure, this reflects again the stereotypes of raters' concepts of behaviour rather than the behaviour of subjects. This argument is supported by evidence that ratings made after subjects seen for a very brief period (such that they could have no factual basis) closely resembled ratings made under normal conditions. However, these claims are again refuted by the evidence. Cattell's (1957) ratings, L data, resemble his Q data, and these self-report questionnaires do, in fact, correlate with a variety of variables. Howarth (1976) has, of course, challenged Cattell's L factors on the grounds that too many factors were extracted and that only five factors subsumed the ratings. However, even if this is so, this does not overturn the original ratings; rather, it changes our understanding of the structure underlying them.

However, in our view all these arguments against traits are refuted by the empirical findings that correlations exist between trait scores and real-life behaviours which can only occur if traits are relatively consistent aspects of human behaviour (see Hogan *et al.*, 1977, for a detailed exposition of this point). These findings will be discussed in the later relevant chapters.

There is a further point devastating to situationalism: biogenetic studies of the hereditary index for many personality traits indicate that much of the population variance is hereditarily determined (Cattell, 1973; Eysenck and Eysenck, 1976).

The kind of evidence adduced by Mischel against a trait psychology, and hence the psychometric model, depends upon experiments conducted with objective tests of highly specific behaviours, as argued by Eysenck and Eysenck (1980). These are influenced more by the situation than are real-life behaviours of real importance to the individual. (Indeed, this point has already been mentioned in our discussions of the limitations of the model.)

In his more recent papers Mischel (e.g. 1977) has, in fact, withdrawn from his more extreme position and is prepared to accept an interactional affect between trait and situation. In the end, therefore, the psychometric model and situationalism differ mainly in the degree of emphasis that they place on traits and situations. Nevertheless, the view of situationalism as having displaced traits (argued by Harré, 1980) cannot be maintained, and this is the critical point of this issue. There is no argument or evidence that, *per se*, renders the psychometric model worthless because it is a trait model.

Conclusions

From this discussion the following conclusions can be drawn.

1 A psychometric model of personality can be drawn utilizing the most important factor analytically defined variables.

2 This model can be tested and developed empirically, thus making it scientific in the sense used by Popper (1959) and useful for theory and practice in psychology.

3 The model does not, *per se*, ignore the influence of situational determinants of behaviour, although as yet the important research into, and measurement of, environmental stimuli has hardly begun.

4 This psychometric model is essentially a trait model, but the influential arguments against trait psychology, current in situationalism, do not render it worthless, since the arguments can be shown to be less than powerful.

5 The differences between the most recent situationalist position and the psychometric model are really ones of emphasis, and they are in no sense antithetical.

6 Finally, it is clear that the psychometric model is a convenient way of utilizing the variables emerging from factor analyses of personality, and, as we have argued throughout this book, this is exactly what should be done with emerging factors, given the power of factor analysis to indicate the most powerful variables.

Summary

1 A psychometric model of personality was described.

2 Its implications and limitations were fully discussed, together with its handling of the environmental determinants of behaviour.

3 Situationalism was described, and its arguments against the trait approach to personality were refuted.

4 It was concluded that the psychometric model of personality is a useful approach to the study of personality.

9 The work of Eysenck and Cattell

In our last chapter a model of personality was proposed, the psychometric model, which, in principle, was able to utilize the most important personality factors in the prediction of behaviour. This was a basic approach to the development of what Cattell calls 'specification equations', and these can be elaborated in a variety of ways in order to accommodate the exigencies of data. Models of this kind are the essence of theories which may be fully developed as efforts are made to account for the observed data of the model.

The two most active workers in the field of factor analysis as applied to personality, Cattell and Eysenck, have developed their own personality theories, each taking account of the main personality factors to have emerged from his own work.

The work of Eysenck

Since the 1940s Eysenck and his colleagues have produced more than fifty books and 300 papers in attempting to establish a factorial basis for personality and to explore the psychological implications of the factors. In addition, much of this work has tested some of the hypotheses to be derived from their theoretical account. For this reason (that of sheer size), our description of this huge corpus of work must do its complexity scant justice. For more detail the best sources are Eysenck (1967) and Eysenck and Eysenck (1976), where comprehensive accounts of the work are to be found.

The basic personality dimensions

These have already been described in Chapter 7, where we set out the factors that must be taken into account in any adequate personality theory (although, of course, the mere fact that a theory does deal with such factors is not in itself sufficient to make it adequate). These were:

1 extraversion – the outgoing, sociable, cheerful, uninhibited dimension;
2 neuroticism – the dimension of worry, nervousness, anxiety and moody instability;
3 psychoticism – the tough-minded, sensation-seeking, inhumane, cruel and antipathetic dimension.

These are orthogonal, independent, temperamental dimensions on the first two of which the majority of individuals are at the mid-point. On psychoticism the distribution is different, the normal individuals scoring low, with high scores characterizing abnormal groups.

The physiological basis for the factors

The fundamental importance of these factors in understanding personality stems in part from the fact that they are behaviour patterns dependent on physiological substrates which are largely genetic in origin. Support for the close association of these factors with physiological systems can be adduced from the fact that biometric studies of the heritability of these factors, as with intelligence, indicates that differences within Western populations can be accounted for by genetic factors (around 70 per cent of the variance is genetically determined) (Eysenck and Eysenck, 1976). Extraversion is related to the excitability of the central nervous system, neuroticism to the lability of the autonomic nervous system and psychoticism to the androgen level of the individual. More specifically, extraversion is seen as reflecting cortical arousal, and this in turn depends upon the activity of the reticular formation. Thus individual differences in extraversion reflect individual differences in reticular formation activity. Similarly, it is the limbic system that is implicated in neuroticism. The physiological basis of P is admitted by Eysenck to be less certain (Eysenck and Eysenck, 1976), but if the relationship to androgen level is confirmed, it is particularly interesting, since androgen level is, of course, related to maleness, and many of the traits of the high-scoring P individual, a psychopathic monster, do in fact characterize that type of criminal offender (of whom Brady is an example) whose members (*pace* Women's Lib.) are rarely women.

If these factors really do have a physiological basis of this kind, there are a number of important psychological implications. The first, that the heritability ratio should be high, for neural structures are little affected by environmental factors other than poisons or other similar accidental damage, we have already discussed; and in fact, this was the case. Again, there should be some overlap between the personality of men and mammals reflecting similarities of physiological organization. To some extent this appears to be the case. Thus Broadhurst (1960) has identified emotionality in rats (as measured by faecal counts – work originated by Hall, 1934), and all three factors have been claimed to be found in monkeys by Chamove *et al.* (1972). This work demonstrates, at least, that Eysenck's claims are not impossible.

Eysenck and his colleagues have attempted to tie E and N into Hullian learning theory and hence into a general theory of behaviour. This is too complex and tendentious a topic to be dealt with here in any detail, but from Eysenck (1967) a summary of his position is possible. We shall deal separately with N and E. P is not yet fully incorporated into such theorizing.

Neuroticism

Although Eysenck admits (1967) that *all* the evidence is not fully supportive, he makes the following claims. Emotion appears to act as drive, and the personality factor, N, refers to the dimension of greater emotional arousability. In emotive situations high emotionality produces high drive, and these emotions (as drive) can either facilitate or hinder performance, depending upon a large number of factors such as drive strength, the difficulty of the task, the individual's previous experience of stress, his intelligence and his status on the other personality factors. Of course, since these cannot be accurately quantified, prediction in the individual case is not yet possible.

A few points can be made about these arguments. There can be little doubt that high emotional arousal affects performance. The public performer, be it of music or sport, or the subject of a driving test or examination is an eloquent witness of this. It seems intuitively correct also that such drive can either hinder or facilitate performance. However, it must be noted in parenthesis that Eysenck (e.g. 1972) objects strongly to those aspects of Freudian theory that predict opposite results as being equally likely, as, for example, in reaction formation. Since, as Eysenck points out, there are obvious interactions with unquantifiable variables such as the individual's previous experience of stress, in substantive terms these claims do not amount to much more than that high N affects performance either for good or for ill. This, however, is important, although many shrewd judges of human nature (with no formal knowledge of psychology) would not be surprised.

Extraversion

Eysenck weaves extraversion into an account of learning, and hence of behaviour, utilizing two further concepts which need to be defined: (a) *inhibition*, physiological inhibition of the cortex referred to by Hull (1943) as reactive inhibition or satiation (the process which enables one not to hear a ticking clock); (b) *excitation*, the opposite of inhibition, a physiological cortical process facilitating almost all mental processes.

These two processes, according to Eysenck (1957), have important implications for personality. First, there is an *individual differences postulate*: there are individual differences in the speed of the dissipation of inhibition. There is also a *topological postulate*: subjects whose excitatory potential is slow and weak are predisposed to develop extraverted behaviour patterns and hysterical neurotic disorders; subjects whose excitatory potential is quick and strong are predisposed to introversion and dysthymia.

Another possible classification is based upon reactive inhibition. The extravert develops inhibition quickly; this is strong and dissipates slowly: in the introvert inhibition is slow to develop and weak, and it dissipates quickly.

Thus, extraversion, linked to these concepts of inhibition and excitation, can be related to psychical fatigue (Eysenck, 1967). For example, on long and tedious jobs there should be clear differences between extraverts and introverts, as inhibition builds up differentially in each group and dissipates or not as the case may be. Thus performance at different points of the job should be distinctive. Extraverts should start better than introverts, do worse in the middle and then improve again. Introverts should produce a far more steady performance. Certainly, studies of such task performance (Eysenck, 1967, 1971) do support this contention.

This section on extraversion can be summarized. Extraversion–introversion seems to be a dimension of behaviour which resembles behaviours considered to be accountable by excitation and inhibition of the central nervous system, more specifically (as we discussed in the section on the physiological basis of the factors) in reticular formation activity. This is the rationale for the implication of extraversion in so diverse a variety of behaviours, for the excitatory–inhibitory process is basic to the activity of the central nervous system.

Evidence for Eysenck's claims

According to Eysenck (1957) these theoretical claims concerning the nature of extraversion have an important and testable implication – namely, that introverts would be expected to condition more quickly than extraverts, and their responses, having been conditioned, should resist extinction longer than those of extraverts. Eysenck (1967) further argues from the postulate concerned with inhibition that this difference in conditionability would be at its largest when the full build-up of inhibition was brought about by the experiment. This proviso concerning the need to allow inhibition to develop is used by Eysenck to explain away the fact that some experiments support the predictions, while others do not. In our view, this argument, although ingenious, is not altogether convincing.

However, there is a further objection to this line of argument which is even more powerful. It assumes, as Vernon (1964) pointed out, that conditionability is a unitary trait – meaning that if one response in a subject is slow to condition, all the other responses are slow, or if a subject is fast for one, he will be fast for all. Now, in fact, such a general trait of conditionability has never been demonstrated (although all that would be required to do so is a factor analysis of the correlations between speeds of conditioning a variety of responses), and the experimental evidence concerning conditioning and extraversion deals mainly with three responses only: verbal conditioning, GSR and eye-blink conditioning.

Indeed, until a general dimension of conditionability is demonstrated, this part of the theory is weak (regardless of any empirical findings with certain responses), especially since Lacey (1967) found in his studies of the indices of activity of the autonomic nervous system that there was no such general reactivity: some individuals responded on GSR, others on heart rate, for example.

Learning and extraversion

As was made clear in our discussion of excitation, this process is held to facilitate not only conditioning in the laboratory, but also learning of the kind obvious in real life. Hence extraversion should be related to learning. However, just as the experimental conditions ensuring a build-up of inhibition are critical for the demonstration of any difference in conditioning between introverts and extraverts, so they are with learning. Since, too, learning in real-life situations is not necessarily bound up with the development of inhibition, extrapolation from laboratory studies to the real world is peculiarly dangerous. In any case, as might be expected, laboratory studies of the relation of extraversion to learning are completely equivocal, although Eysenck (1967), through speculative arguments of the kind suggested, does manage to fit the results into his framework that extraversion tends to make learning less efficient when the conditions facilitating inhibition are present.

One study by Mohan and Kumar (1976) in the Punjab indicates the relation of extraversion to learning tasks in the real world. They selected introverts and extraverts, using the Punjabi EPI, and investigated the performance of these groups on Raven's Matrices, so that strictly it was a study of performance rather than learning *per se*, although its relevance is to learning. Extraverts started well and declined. Introverts improved over the course of the test, as predicted from Eysenckian theory. This finding may well account for the small but positive correlation that is regularly found between introversion and academic performance at the secondary and tertiary levels (e.g. Kline, 1966a). However, even this is not the simplest hypothesis. One of the EPI items concerns liking reading, and many concern not liking parties. Hence it may be simply that introverts are studious, quiet individuals and hence better at exams. There is no need to invoke cortical inhibition and excitation.

Given that the results by Mohan and Kumar are generalizable to tasks other than the completion of the matrices, they suggest that introverts and extraverts should adopt different strategies of learning: spaced practice for extraverts, massed for introverts, short periods for extraverts, long periods for introverts and so on. However, since factors other than temperament (e.g. dynamic factors of interest) influence learning, such strategies are not likely to have powerful effects in real life.

We have not discussed the large corpus of experimental findings on the relation of extraversion and learning (fully surveyed and scrutinized in Eysenck, 1967), not only because the results are equivocal, with about half the experiments supporting the theoretical predictions, but also because there are a number of problems in the theory itself. These we shall now briefly mention.

First, there is an additional aspect to consolidation theory

(Eysenck, 1976) which attempts to subsume the effects on learning of the arousal produced by the material to be learned and the consolidation of the memory trace. That there is such an effect is clearly shown by the work of Kleinsmith and Kaplan (1963, 1964): high-arousal words were poorly recalled at first, but a week later there was improvement, whereas with low-arousal words the opposite was the case.

In an attempt to explain the results of experiments linking extraversion to learning, Eysenck invokes consolidation theory, but in doing so he creates a dreadful confusion, as we have pointed out (Kline, 1979). Thus he claims that stimulus-produced arousal may be hypothesized to have effects similar to states of 'excitation/arousal'. The words in quotation marks constitute the difficulty. As stated in the 1967 account, arousal and excitation are separate. Excitation–inhibition refers to processes in the central nervous system related to extraversion–introversion, as we have seen. Arousal refers in the theory to the autonomic nervous system. The factor implicated here is not E but N, neuroticism, orthogonal to extraversion. Thus the linking of excitation and arousal is not permitted by the theory.

Indeed, the variations of inhibition, excitation, arousal, together with consolidation, are so complex that prediction becomes almost impossible and *post hoc* explanation almost always possible (not the mark of a good or useful theory).

If this attack on the complexity and incoherence of the theory is not particularly powerful, Reid (1960) has demonstrated some fundamental theoretical inadequacies such that it is difficult to take the theory seriously at all, although most psychologists seem to have ignored Reid's points. The first difficulty raised by Reid is that the theory of inhibition–excitation fails to account for the build up of inhibition. For example, when involuntary rest pauses occur, reinforcement due to resting is supposed to generate conditioned inhibition. However, in conditioned eye-blink experiments, there is no time for such involuntary pauses. That being the case, how can extinction take place? Reid also notes that Eysenck argues that conditioned inhibition is unreinforced and hence extinguished where no rest pauses occur. However, this inhibition is not a response and thus cannot be reinforced or extinguished. Although Reid raises other objections to the theory, these two are sufficient for our point: this attempt by Eysenck to weave extraversion into a theory of learning is not wholly successful.

Indeed, in conclusion all that can be said is that N and E do affect learning in some instances, but as yet a convincing theoretical account of this has not been suggested. Despite these problems with Eysenck's theorizing, however, on one criterion of the worth of a theory it must be judged successful. It has stimulated a huge body of research and writing.

The work of Cattell

Cattell has also attempted to utilize his factors in a theory of personality. His attempt, indeed, is ambitious in the extreme, since it embraces ability, temperament, dynamics, states and situations, as was indicated in our chapter on the psychometric model. Although the specification equation, a psychometric model, summarizes this theoretical account, what Cattell's theorizing does is to explicate the model.

Cattell (1980) has set out his final grand theory, *Personality and Learning Theory* in two volumes: which together run to 1064 pages. Furthermore, by any criteria these books are difficult. Thus to summarize Cattellian theory adequately in the brief space of this chapter is beyond the powers of this writer. However, what can be done is to select the most important parts of his theory, and those that are best based on evidence, and to examine these. We shall, therefore, examine those aspects of Cattell's work which make most use of the factored test variables and which bear also on issues that are central to the understanding of personality.

As co-author with Cattell of *The Scientific Analysis of Personality and Motivation* (Cattell and Kline, 1977), a book which summarized Cattell's work on personality, we feel in a favoured position to make this necessarily somewhat arbitrary selection of topics. An essential concept of Cattell's theoretical approach is his notion of integration learning, itself a part of his structured learning theory. Since learning is clearly central to the understanding of human behaviour, this is a convenient point of entry into Cattell's work.

Integration learning

Integration learning aims to maximize satisfaction by ensuring maximum overall reduction in ergic tension (ergs are the Cattellian drives). Essentially, this operationally defines reinforcement. Just as

Hull (1943) saw reinforcement as drive (anxiety) reduction, this is also Cattell's view, except that it is the reduction over all ergs, not just one, that is important.

To exemplify the point a sexual example may be taken. The immediate satisfaction of sexual drive can lead to the frustration of self-sentiment and super-ego ergs. Sexual satisfaction in our society has to await an appropriate time and place. Self-sentiment would be frustrated for most individuals if they were seen as child molesters or seducers of young girls; their self-esteem would be lowered. Similarly, their guilt would be high. Ultimately, indeed, if their sexual acts were illegal, their capacity for satisfactory tension reduction would be heavily reduced by their residence in prison.

Thus to ensure maximal overall satisfaction of ergic tension, gratification of one drive has to be delayed for the sake of the others. This, in fact, is achieved through the two sentiments which in our example above were so clearly involved – super-ego and self-sentiment. It is through the satisfaction of these drives that the maximal satisfaction of the other drives is attained. Integration learning is the process by which we learn to modify our efforts to drive reduction. This aspect of the theory resembles the claims of McDougall (1932), who referred to self-sentiment as the master sentiment. It is not dissimilar to psychoanalytic theory, which sees maturity as that period when the ego, the reality principle, can control the id (the pleasure principle) just enough to allow for proper drive expression but without offending the super-ego. Cattell's integration learning, therefore, has a sound historical clinical basis but can, unlike earlier clinical theories, be operationalized in terms of equations (the dynamic calculus) and variables, the MAT (see p. 89) measuring the major drives.

Cattell (1965), in an attempt to show how integration learning works, produced what he called the 'adjustment process analysis (APA) chart'. This can be quantified into a dynamic calculus. This adjustment process simply supposes that as a drive is barred satisfaction, a number of possible actions lie open to an individual. Depending on his choice, further barriers may be raised, and there will be a further choice point. This process continues until the drive either finds expression or is repressed entirely. What choice we make at each point depends on the development of our super-ego and self-sentiment. Our choices affect observable behaviour, so that a good understanding of this adjustment process should lead to a good understanding of behaviour of personality.

However, readers must beware! This APA chart is only an illustration of what might happen when a given drive is stimulated. In this sense it is no different from, say, the psychoanalytic descriptions of defence mechanism-mediated behaviour. Despite the fact, therefore, that attempts to put it into mathematical terms have been made by Cattell and Child (1975) – what they call the multi-dimensional learning matrix – this part of Cattell's theory, although utilizing known ergs, is purely speculative. However, it does illustrate how the factored variables can be built up into theories.

This multi-dimensional learning matrix assumes that any given activity, if goal-directed, is likely to produce small changes in personality factors, and the algebra purports to be able to calculate these changes (and hence test the theory), although again there is almost no empirical work to support these claims. In everyday life it is clear that such changes do occur. For example, a librarian is likely to become quieter than he was on account of his work; old schoolmasters and doctors can be recognized.

Cattell (1980) has developed a structured learning theory which makes much use of this algebraic approach (which is indeed its basis) and has produced what seems to us an entirely new model of personality, which takes account of the factor-analytic variables that have emerged from his studies and are discussed fully in the relevant chapters of our book. It differs from Cattell's previous attempts to synthesize his findings in that it takes account of systems theory. This model is formidably complex, and all we can do here is present some of its main features. It stands as a monument to Cattell's prodigious efforts in the field of personality over a period of almost fifty years. However, it must be emphasized that this model is not buttressed by powerful empirical findings, although the variables it uses are clearly defined at least in Cattell's own work.

The VIDAS model (Cattell, 1980)

The basic essentials of the VIDAS model are:

1 reservoirs of information and energy – each reservoir has a particular type of content and is of finite size, and there are individual differences in respect of such limits;
2 channels of varying capacity between the subsystems of reservoirs;
3 positive and negative feedback loops between the subsystems;
4 reversible and irreversible transformations;

5 hierarchical structure of the subsystems such that some control others;
6 decoding and encoding units for transforming stimuli in the world and for the storage of information within the systems – in effect, transducers.

These six essentials are necessary for any information-processing model, not just for a model of personality. They could be built into a machine, and this is what the field of artificial intelligence is broadly concerned with.

Before seeing how this very general description of the VIDAS model is applied specifically to a model of human personality, there are a few points about it that need to be stressed, as Cattell (1980) argues. There is a difficulty in the model concerning just what is supposed to flow through the channels. A biological model of the organism would clearly be concerned with physical matter (hormones and enzymes, for example), and there would be no intrinsic difficulty. Similarly, a computer simulation of behaviour, as used in the studies of artificial intelligence (e.g. Boden, 1977), deals largely with information. This again presents no problem, since information is readily quantified, as in computers, into bits. However, in some systems, as in engineering, what is transmitted through the system is energy. In such systems the transmission of energy presents no conceptual difficulty. Energy can be transformed (there are electrical and chemical equivalents, for example), as in a hydro-electric system or indeed in a simple battery.

For a psychological model, however, the concept of energy is a major problem. Behaviourists (e.g. Skinner, 1953) have abandoned the notion because it cannot be operationally defined or measured, although the majority of theories concerned with human behaviour have found it necessary. Cattell also feels forced to use it in the VIDAS system, and attempts to define it as reactivity to stimuli. However, as Cattell admits, this just will not do, since a silent, thinking man solving a problem of great complexity may be utilizing far more energy than a noisy football fan. Cattell attempts to operationalize his definition by using the total interest score on measures of ergs and sentiments. In any case, in the model both energy and information units are transmitted.

The VIDAS model is, then, basically a standard systems analytic model with cybernetic controls and deals with information and energy applied to behaviour. How it is applied in fact, the details which distinguish it from a model of some other system, will now be considered. This discussion of the details of the VIDAS model will be brief, for several reasons. From the viewpoint of our book, the interest in the VIDAS model springs from the basic systems analytic approach. The detailed application is only one way in which the approach could be operationalized – Cattell's way. Now this, although impressive, is frankly speculative, as Cattell (1980) admits, and given the generality of the model, a whole variety of such detailed descriptive models could probably be drawn up. Which one turned out to be the best, given that their assumptions and coherence were the same, would depend on how well empirical findings fitted the model. Since there are no such research findings, however, the development of so detailed a model is a purely speculative tribute to the imagination rather than an account of knowledge.

There are seven components within the system:

1 an input handling system (this handles ingoing data from the perceptual apparatus);
2 an ergic need system (this stores the results of the stimulation of ergic needs);
3 M – Engram or memory storage;
4 general states; these respond to perception of success and failure to ergic levels and to ego control;
5 the trait properties of the organism – abilities and temperament;
6 the control system;
7 machinery for the execution of response.

Cattell claims that current research into ergs, traits and abilities supports this system, although he admits that for the proper demonstration of the model the 'simple', multivariate approach is no longer sufficient. However, the methods he advocates have never been used, and only future research will be able to evaluate the power of the Vidas model.

We have discussed the VIDAS model because it is an important part of Cattell's final synthesis of his research findings into a theory of personality. It is an attempt to do what we have been advocating throughout this book. However, in our view it is premature in the light of the current state of knowledge. We prefer Cattell's far more elementary approach in constructing specification equations for behaviours, as described in our chapter on the psychometric model. These equations make use of all the factors and, if yielding high indices, have empirical support. When enough of these equations have been formulated, then it may be useful to try to build a theory to account for the results.

Systems analytic models stand or fall, it seems to us, on how well results can be predicted from them. To construct a model which is in advance of the algebra and experimental data needed to check it, on principles of model construction, does not seem to us valuable in that there is no evidence at present either in support of or against the model. A magnificent intellectual effort, but an effort that needs substantiation by data.

Conclusions

The work of Eysenck and Cattell is notable for its extent and scope. Yet, as we have seen, quite apart from any problems over their original database, neither theory can really command support. Both attempt what needs to be done, however. Any criticisms are not intended to belittle their work: they reflect the immense difficulty of the task of constructing a theory of personality based upon quantified variables.

Summary

1 Two theoretical accounts of the factorial results, those of Eysenck and Cattell, were described.
2 Eysenck's theories were examined:
   (a) the physiology;
   (b) the implication of E and N in theories of learning via inhibition and excitation;
   (c) criticisms of the theorizing.
3 The work of Cattell was examined:
   (a) integration learning;
   (b) the dynamic calculus and the multi-dimensional learning matrix;
   (c) structured learning;
   (d) the VIDAS model.

10 Measurement and clinical theories of personality

In this chapter we shall discuss the findings described in earlier chapters, those derived from psychological tests of demonstrated reliability and validity, as they relate to clinical theories of personality. 'Clinical' is a term that we here use in an extended sense, referring not only to theories whose origin lies in clinical observation as is the case with almost all varieties of psychoanalytic theory, but also to theories that are based on data collected by methods similar to those used in clinics. The outstanding example of this is Murray's (1938) work, known as personology. In any case such theorizing is usually heavily dependent on clinical data that are implicit (that is, they exist in the mind of the theorist).

There have been a huge number of attempts to define personality and to theorize about it, so that in a single chapter it is not possible to discuss all such theories. Clearly, a selection has to be made. We have surveyed some leading personality texts; almost all of these have chapters on Freud and some other analysts, so that these are even now regarded as influential. We are therefore going to discuss these theories in relation to the psychometric results. In addition, we consider psychoanalytic theories to be among the most powerful in the field, despite their severe critics. Among the other theorists whom we examine our selection is more arbitrary. We look at the work of Murray because his theories are used as a basis for a number of psychological tests (as we saw in Chapter 4) and because one of his own tests, the TAT, is still in use by those who favour projective methods. Furthermore, personology as an approach seems to us to have been neglected in recent psychology, partly because it is somewhat subjective and partly because it is difficult to collect the necessary data – it simply takes more time than most subjects are prepared to give.

First, we shall examine the psychometric findings in relation to psychoanalytic theories.

Extraversion

As we saw, extraversion is one of the two largest factors to emerge from questionnaires. Jung (1923), the founder of analytical psychology and the heir to Freud – who broke with him because of Freud's insistence on pan-sexuality (although indubitably personal differences between them made some contribution to the schism) – regarded extraversion as a highly important aspect of personality. He claimed that individuals fall into two groups, distinguished by their orientation. The introvert is oriented inwards, interested in feelings and his inner self; the extravert, on the other hand, is concerned with the outer world. For him feelings are unimportant. This, however, is not all. In addition to orientation, there are four modes of operation, of which one is usually paramount in each individual. These four modes are: thinking, feeling, intuiting and sensing. In philosophers and mathematicians, to exemplify the modes, thinking is primary. Where feeling is the mode, the individual is characterized by strong emotions – A. E. Housman is perhaps a typical feeling introvert. The individual in whom sensations are paramount when extraverted is the archetypal country squire, happy only when killing something, and that preferably eatable. When introverted he is the connoisseur; the man who can discriminate the Maduras Havana from the Colorado. The intuitive types are the mystics: Blake and Hitler (similar at least in this).

Although the factor-analytic work makes it clear that in seizing upon extraversion–introversion as a major temperamental variable, Jung was correct, there are some important differences between the factor-analytic and the Jungian concepts. One of these, the most critical, concerns the nature of extraversion. In Jungian theory this is a typology. An individual is either an extravert or an introvert. If this were so, there should be a bimodal distribution of scores on measures of extraversion. In the factor-analytic work, however, extraversion–introversion is a dimension, a continuum, with the majority of the population around the mean of a normal distribution. A further distinction between the factorial and Jungian concepts is that in the factorial work there is almost no evidence for the modes of operation. It is perhaps just possible to argue that social and thinking extraversion are equivalent to the feeling and thinking modes and that impulsivity (which in Eysenck's EPI was part of extraversion) is similar to the sensory mode. However, this is not convincing. Finally, it should be noted that two tests claiming to measure the eight Jungian types have been developed – the Myers–Briggs Type Indicator (Briggs and Myers, 1962), and the Gray–Wheelwright Inventory (Gray and Wheelwright, 1946).

In conclusion, then, it can be argued that one concept of Jungian theory, that which emphasizes the importance of extraversion in understanding personality, is supported by the factor-analytic work. However, the concepts are not identical, and it was to avoid precisely this confusion that Cattell preferred to label his extraversion factor 'exvia'.

Neuroticism

We must now discuss the relevance to psychoanalytic theories of the second large personality factor, neuroticism or anxiety. As with extraversion, this is a dimension, on which most normals score around the mean or lower. The significance of a very low score is not clear. One clear inference concerning neurosis that can be drawn from the nature of this factor is that neurotics (who score high on N) are not qualitatively different from normals. It would appear that there is no basic difference between the personalities of normals and neurotics; one is an extreme form of the other. Such an inference is, of course, in line with psychoanalytic theories. One of the undeniable legacies from these theories is the now almost universally held belief that neurotics are not different from normals. Psychoanalysis to some extent helped banish the fear, awe and hatred of the mentally ill, who once (and, alas, in some ecclesiastical quarters things have not changed) were seen as evil and diabolically possessed. In psychoanalytic theory neurotic symptoms are basically seen as defences. Now, all normals also defend, but not so often or so vigorously, hence the quantitative rather than qualitative differences. Neurosis is an exaggeration of normal behaviour. To this extent, the N factor is in accord with psychoanalytic theory. It cannot, however, be regarded as powerful support. At least it is not a refutation.

Psychoticism

The P factor, it will be remembered, distinguishes psychotics from normals and neurotics. On this factor these groups score extremely low. Almost alone the psychotic and the psychopath have elevated scores. Eysenck and Eysenck (1976) have attempted to argue that the quantitative differences implied by this P factor between psychotics and others refutes psychoanalytic theory. This, however, is not so. The psychotic, according to Freud (1924), denies reality and obeys the instinct, whereas the neurotic denies the instinct and obeys reality. Thus in the theory there is discontinuity between the psychotic, and normals and neurotics. In the psychotic the defences have broken down, and primary process thinking has taken over and may be acted out. Thus, on the contrary, the fact that P discriminates psychotics from others who score low on the factor is quite consistent with the theory. Again, as was the case with N, the factorial work supports the general psychoanalytic approach to mental illness but provides no confirmation of any of the more specific hypothesis.

The Cattell primary factors

In terms of nomenclature, the Cattell primary factors – despite the problems of their factorial clarity (see Chapter 7) – would appear to support the Freudian hypotheses concerning the dimension of the mind (id, ego and super-ego), since there are three factors by that name: C, ego strength; G, super-ego; and Q4, id tension. However, we must not be misled by these names, since Cattell was himself influenced by psychoanalytic theory in thus labelling them.

Nevertheless, examination of the scores of neurotic groups on these factors (results which we also discuss in the next chapter, on the application of these findings) does in part support psychoanalytic theory. In that theory neurotics are supposed to have weak egos, hence their problems in defending against the id drives. Their super-egos (i.e. their feelings of guilt) are reputed to be high (Freud, 1924). In fact, examination of the 16PF scores of clinical groups reported in the technical handbook to the test (Cattell *et al.*, 1970a) shows that C was low in all neurotic patients and that, interestingly enough, it rose with lobotomized patients. When we consider the behaviour patterns of the low-scoring on factor C – easily annoyed, feels dissatisfied, runs into emotional problems, collects difficulties (Cattell and Kline, 1977) – it is clear that Freudian theory is supported by the implication of this factor in neurosis.

On the other hand, factor G (super-ego), the conscientious rule-bound, dimension, is not high in neurotics as predicted by psychoanalytic theory. Thus Freud's claim that the severity of the super-ego plays a causative role in the aetiology of the neuroses is not confirmed. There are two interesting points to be noted about this finding. First, although G (super-ego) is not high, factor O (guilt proneness), is always elevated among neurotic groups. Thus guilt feelings do seem to be associated with neuroses. The high-scoring (O) subject is described by Cattell and Kline (1977) as having few friends, being critical of group life and standards, suffering from a generalized feeling of inadequacy and loneliness. The second point is concerned with Mowrer's (1950) hypothesis that neurotics are not high on super-ego but low (i.e. that they are guilty). This, however, is not confirmed by these data, since on G neurotics score around the normal mean. Freudian theory is not supported, therefore, by these findings, although guilt is implicated in neurosis.

Q4 (id tension) is high in neurotic groups, and this is consonant with psychoanalytic theory in the light of Freud's claim concerning the aims of his therapy: where id was, there shall ego be. Thus the findings with Q4 support, to some extent, the Freudian formulation of the mind and its relation to neurotic disorders.

Two more researches deserve brief mention at this point. Warburton (1968) factored the 16PF scales to the fourth order and extracted two factors, morality (loading on G) v. thrust. This resembles the ego–super-ego conflict of psychoanalytic theory. However, this was a small-scale study, and the rotation was far from precise, with few points (at this high order, without grounded primaries) against which to locate the factors.

Pawlik and Cattell (1964) carried out a third-order factor analysis of objective personality tests, from which the three emerging factors were labelled ego, super-ego and id. However, given the problems concerning the validity of these objective tests (see Chapter 5), the labelling of broad third-orders is fraught with difficulty. As we have previously argued, far more research into the nature and validity of objective tests is required before any confident identification of factors can be undertaken.

Thus in respect of Freudian theory a degree of support may be said to arise from the work of Cattell, despite its problems, in the field of temperament. The conceptualization of mental activity as subsumed by three structures, id, ego and super-ego, is not entirely wide of the mark. Clearly, though, hypotheses concerning the nature and action of the super-ego require modification in the light of the factor-analytic findings.

Other factor-analytic solutions

In our chapter on the factor analysis of personality questionnaires we discussed the work of Grygier (1961, 1976), whose DPI test claimed to measure psychosexual variables such as orality and narcissism. These are aspects of Freudian psychosexual theory (Freud, 1905), in which it is claimed that oral, anal and phallic characters are derived from fixation at the relevant developmental levels. Kline has discussed all this work in great detail (Kline, 1972, 1981) and has carried out extensive research into these personality syndromes (e.g. Kline, 1969, 1980a, 1980b), and we shall here merely summarize the general conclusions that may be drawn from these studies.

It can be argued on the basis of the factor-analytic work that two syndromes of personality, oral optimistic and oral pessimistic character, which resemble the psychoanalytic descriptions, do appear to emerge (Kline and Storey, 1977). However, their relationship to anything that might be called oral is more dubious, although Kline and Storey (1980) found relationships between these scores with smoking, food preferences and nail biting. The aetiology of the oral character demands, therefore, further and more detailed research, ideally a combination of statistical and clinical methods.

As regards the anal character, the evidence is far less equivocal. Kline (1971) developed a measure of this Ai3Q, which repeatedly (e.g. Kline, 1967, 1978) loads upon an obsessional trait factor independent of the Cattell and Eysenck factors. Thus it can be argued that a personality constellation similar to that of the anal character emerges. Again, its relationship to anality has not been demonstrated, although Kline (1968) found that Ai3Q scores related to the anal pictures of Blum's (1949) Blacky Pictures.

There seems to be no evidence for the phallic character – at least no writer has been able to develop a scale of such characteristics. In conclusion, then, the factor-analytic evidence from tests supports Freud's observations that various personality syndromes could be noted. However, the claims linking them to pregenital eroticism, whence their names were derived, have not yet convincingly been confirmed.

Relevance of the dynamic factors to psychoanalytic theory

The factor analysis of motivation gave rise to sets of factors: one was concerned with strength of interest, of which there were seven components, three of which were named, ego, super-ego and id. The second set was concerned with the main drives underlying human behaviour.

The strength-of-interest factors

The fact that the three largest of these factors were given psychoanalytic titles means (at the least) that to Cattell and his colleagues there appeared to be a resemblance between these factors and the Freudian concepts. However, examination of these factors (which are difficult to identify from their factor loadings because they are T, objective-test factors, which by definition are not face-valid), suggests that the identification must not be taken too literally. The alpha factor is actually called 'conscious id'. Eysenck (1972) has objected to this label on the grounds that it is nonsensical, since the id is unconscious. This is true, of course, although Cattell calls it 'conscious id' precisely to differentiate it from the Freudian concept and to highlight its resemblances (i.e. the 'I desire' component of the factor even against one's better judgement). This is particularly obvious in purchasing, when most people have experienced the drive to buy something even though they knew it to be unsuitable. Beta and gamma are closer to their psychoanalytic counterparts, but the approximation is admitted by Cattell (1957) and Cattell and Child (1975) to be rough. The point of the names was not that they were precisely like the Freudian concepts but that psychoanalytic theory was the only existing framework which could accommodate, even loosely, these particular factors.

From this it can be concluded, therefore, that the strength-of-interest factors support the general psychoanalytic approach to dynamics (that is, there is an interplay of components in strength of interest) rather than confirm in detail the psychoanalytic hypotheses.

At the second order, it will be remembered, two factors, integrated and unintegrated components, account for the variance. To some extent these resemble ego and id, since the integrated factor is reality-based, while the unintegrated component reflects spontaneous interests below the level of our awareness.

However, the fit is far from precise, and the factor-analytic findings, which in any case are somewhat primitive at the present state of research, give only modest and general support for this aspect of psychoanalytic theorizing.

The ergs and sentiments

On the question of drives, it is possible to derive two hypotheses from Freudian theory, which, it must be remembered, was never static but was in a perpetual state of development as new data arrived. The most usual Freudian approach suggests strongly that we should find paramount two drives, sex and aggression. Later formulations, however, hypothesize the life and death instincts as all-important. Fenichel (1945) argues that few analysts have taken this later almost metaphysical speculation seriously, although Fromm (1974) makes use of it in understanding the psychology of Hitler, and Melanie Klein (1948) by no means ignores it.

In fact, the emergence of five sentiments and five ergs does not confirm the psychoanalytic hypotheses. The factor-analytic results show more drives to be necessary in accounting for behaviour than Freud suggested, although sex and aggression are important. However, psychoanalytic theory is certainly not needed to hypothesize the significance of these drives.

As regards Eros and Thanatos, nothing in the factor-analytic work comes near to supporting these claims; indeed, it is difficult to know just what evidence could confirm them. In brief, the factor-analytic work indicates that Freud underestimated the number and variety of human drives.

However, before writing off this part of Freudian theory one point must be noted. Sexuality, as used by Freud, is a broad concept, far broader than the normal notion of sexuality involving adult genital behaviour. Aggression also denotes a wide variety of feelings and behaviours so that factor analytically these should appear as higher-order factors. Since the higher-order structure of these ergs and sentiments is not fully worked out – studies by Burdsall (e.g. 1975) indicate unstable factor structures at the first order, as did the study by Cooper and Kline (1982) – it could still turn out that Freud's claims as to the supreme importance of aggression and sexuality were correct. At present, however, the evidence is not in his favour.

In conclusion, therefore, it can be seen that the psychometric findings do not support Freudian theory in any detail, although they are consonant in some cases with its broad approach. The emphasis given by Jung to extraversion is supported by psychometric work, although extraversion is a continuum, and the typological claims are not confirmed.

The work of Murray

Murray (1938) described what he called personology in *The Exploration of Personality*. This involved the detailed study of interviews, essays, biographies and projective- and questionnaire-test responses, *inter alia*, and, of course, a great deal of interpretation based upon explicit and implicit theories of personality. Murray's dedication in his book was to Jung, and there can be no missing his essentially psychoanalytic orientation. Nevertheless, his own theoretical structure conceptualized human dynamics in terms of needs and presses which were the environmental influences relevant to these needs.

Murray postulated that about twenty-five needs underlie human behaviour (at least in the West), and one of his projective tests, the TAT, specifically designed to tap these needs and their corresponding presses, is still widely used, even though alternative scoring procedures not involving needs are sometimes used. As we indicated earlier in this chapter, some leading psychologists involved in the measurement of personality, Edwards and Jackson, have used Murray's dynamic framework as a basis for item writing and test selection, so that it is pertinent to inquire to what extent the best validated factored results support Murray's work.

First, the fact that Murray claimed so many needs to be important is not supported by the factor-analytic evidence. Whereas, as we have seen, Freud seems to underestimate the variety of human motivation, Murray has exaggerated it. As we have argued (Cattell and Kline, 1977), it could be the case that Murray isolated surface traits, observably syndromes of behaviour, rather than the source traits underlying them.

However, since Edwards and Jackson have both developed questionnaire tests to measure these needs (discussed in Chapters 3 and 6), it might be argued that, *ipso facto*, this is evidence that needs are useful concepts: if something exists, it must exist in some quantity and can, therefore, be measured. This argument will not do, however. First (as was pointed out in Chapter 6), there is no evidence supporting the validity of these scales. Their validity (although superbly constructed) derives from little more than face validity. Furthermore, the method of scale construction was not such as would inevitably result in the emergence of dynamic (as distinct from temperamental) factors, the reason why these tests were also discussed in our chapter on temperamental traits. Thus although the tests are carefully constructed, their lack of evidence of validity does not make their actual existence support for the theory. In brief, Murray's theorizing is not supported by the factorial work.

Before we finally leave the work of Murray, we must mention briefly the work on achievement motivation, the need to achieve (Nach). In his original work this was measured by the TAT. However, the importance attached by some psychologists to reliable measurement caused them to abandon the TAT measure and to develop questionnaires – Hundal (1970) and Lynn (1969), for example, both of whom have demonstrated that questionnaire measures of Nach are higher in entrepreneurs than in controls in big companies, in various cultures. Such research, of course, followed the work of McClelland (1961), who has attempted to study Nach in a variety of cultures at various points in their development. Indeed, he concludes that this variable is an important determinant of a high-achieving society.

Since there is some evidence that Nach is associated with achievement among both individuals and societies, it becomes pertinent to ask why this variable has not appeared in the factor-analytic work, and why it has not been included in our list of variables that deserve further study. Cattell and Child (1975) supply part of the answer to this question. They argue that Nach is a surface trait (i.e. it is not factor-pure). It loads on career, self-assertion and self-sentiment. To study it properly it is better to study these variables separately. The other argument which runs against the Nach variables is that the various measures of it are not well correlated. Thus results derived from studies in which one particular measure has been used are by no means applicable to studies in which other tests are employed. As Fineman (1977) points out, this lack of agreement between the various measures of Nach means that as a variable it has not been properly operationally defined. It is, of course, inevitable that unless they are deliberately developed with controls over the proportions of variance accounted for by factors, multi-factored variables will not correlate highly among themselves.

Thus, although Murray was accurate in observing Nach as an important syndrome, it is clear that it is better measured by tests of its component factors. In conclusion, it can be seen that Murray's variables, based on acute inferences from clinical-like data, fall far short of the statistically defined variables emerging from factor analysis. This supports Meehl's (1954) claim that clinical judgements cannot match statistical decisions.

The work of McDougall

A brief mention must be made of the work of McDougall because his motivational framework (McDougall, 1932) was taken over by Cattell in the interpretation of the motivational factors. Thus McDougall listed eighteen main propensities, 'the mainsprings of all human . . . activity'. However, he argued that the sentiments are more important energizers, for it is within these that the propensities are organized in man. In fact – and this is the reason why Cattell adopted the framework – the factorial results do appear to fit these claims: ergs are equivalent to propensities, and the sentiments are highly similar in both systems. In our chapter on motivation and integration learning the importance of the self-sentiment and super-ego in the reduction of ergic tension was stressed and this again, the notion of a master sentiment, was taken over from McDougall.

However, before concluding that modern factor-analytic studies of human dynamics confirm the early speculative psychology, two points must be noted. Careful examination of Cattell and Child shows that the identification and validity of these dynamic factors is still tentative. There is far less evidence supporting them than is the case with the best-known temperamental factors. This being the case, the labelling of these factors must be regarded as recognition that they broadly resemble the propensities and sentiments of McDougall and that at present this is the nearest theoretical exposition into which they could fit. More precise identification will not be possible until more is known about these factors; until this point all interpretations and identifications must be duly cautious.

Conclusions

We have compared the factored psychometric personality test results with some well-known theories of personality that have posited similar variables. It is concluded that these theories did contain valuable insights, as might be expected, but clinical observation and inference is necessarily inferior to the statistically based inferences that can be made from multivariate analysis *provided that the database (i.e. the test items) of such analyses is satisfactory*. This does not mean that such clinically based theories are worthless. On the contrary, where they deal with data that as yet defies accurate measurement (as psychoanalysis does), they will contain important hypotheses untouched by multivariate studies. This is why the development of good tests is so important, especially that of projective tests, which can handle such data and yet yield quantitative results.

Summary

1 Psychometric findings and their impact on clinical theories of personality were discussed and examined:
   (a) extraversion and its relation to Jungian theory
   (b) neuroticism and its relation to the psychoanalytic theory of neurosis.
2 Psychoticism was discussed in the same way.
3 The Cattell primary factors and other factorial solutions were examined.
4 Dynamic factors were discussed. It was concluded that in general rather than in detail, some aspects of psychoanalytic theory were confirmed.
5 The work of Murray and McDougall was discussed in the light of the findings.
6 Broadly, all these theories received a small degree of support, but it was argued that they were inferior to multivariate analyses, given the construction of good tests.

11 Application of the findings in clinical, educational and occupational psychology

We have decided it best to treat the application of the findings from the testing of personality in educational, clinical and occupational psychology as one topic. This is because all these branches of applied psychology have problems, solutions and theories in common. Clearly, these may be dealt with together. Such a method will also reveal differences and distinctive aspects of these applied subjects, which can be discussed as they arise.

Boundaries and definitions

Educational psychology can be defined as concerned with psychological factors affecting educational performance. In a similar way, clinical psychology is the study of psychological factors affecting mental health, while industrial psychology is concerned with the welfare and efficiency of workers. As we have argued elsewhere (Kline, 1979), in all these fields, the problems fall into neat categories.

Diagnosis and treatment

This is an aspect of both clinical and educational psychology and, to a lesser extent, of occupational psychology. Some examples will clarify this point. A child with difficulties in reading may be referred to an educational psychologist. Diagnosis of the causes of the problem is desirable, as is treatment. Either, in fact, may be possible. Thus a carefully structured teaching programme might remedy the fault without ever finding the cause. Similarly, the cause might be known but all treatment might be unsuccessful. In clinical psychology treatment and diagnosis are far more obvious, although it must be noted that behaviour therapists are usually uninterested in diagnosis, regarding the symptoms as the problem and essentially enabling the patient to unlearn the maladaptive learning and to relearn more appropriate responses. In occupational psychology this class of problem would include the cases of workers (including management) who found their jobs stressful and difficult and whose problems could be identified. Here an attempt would be made to find the causes of the problems and, having found them, to treat them.

Assessment procedures

Although the *Zeitgeist* assumes that assessment procedures are bad, it should be clear that, prejudice apart, for certain courses in education and for certain occupations special qualities are necessary, and hence assessment is important. The aim of assessment is to find the right people, those most suitable for the task in hand. In clinical psychology assessment is mainly diagnostic in character, and it may be an artificial distinction for this branch of psychology.

Guidance and counselling

This is an important aspect of all three applied psychologies, in which it is often helpful to discuss problems and difficulties with those concerned. Vocational guidance and counselling is a special form of these procedures, most commonly used in educational institutions and large organizations, although even in the clinic, where disease may affect job prospects, it can be important. In some instances, of course, the distinction between counselling and treatment is slight. This should not be allowed to blur a genuine difference.

Theory

In all these three applied fields there is a desperate need for adequate theories. For example, no theory of instruction exists such that teachers can be trained rationally. Again, in the field of clinical psychology no fully accepted theory is used by practitioners. Certainly, a large number of clinical theories abound, but each is held in contempt by adherents of other theories. Similarly, there is no sound theoretical account that might help people to understand job satisfaction and success.

This analysis of the applied fields of psychology (educational, occupational and clinical) as four categories of problems or work does, it seems, cover most of what is or could be done in these areas. In some cases (as, for example, that of diagnosis and assessment in clinical psychology) the distinction is fine, perhaps arbitrary.

Generally, however, each category involves the solution of different problems, and thus the value and power of the psychometric approach to personality will be different for each category.

In this chapter we shall examine the contribution that the measurement of personality and motivation, as discussed in this book, has made to the different aspects of applied psychology. In addition, we shall scrutinize the contribution that it could and should make, for it is indubitably the case that at present this approach to personality is heavily undervalued not only by practitioners, of course, but also, as we have seen, by academic specialists in the field. However, many of their claims (e.g. situationalism) we have already rebutted (see Chapter 8), and as we discuss the topics in this chapter it will become clear that the psychometric approach is still vigorous. In a chapter of this length we shall have to be selective and shall examine those aspects of applied psychology, as categorized above, on which psychometrics has made the most notable impact.

Assessment is the field in which the psychometric approach to personality has the most to offer, and with this we shall begin our discussion.

Educational assessment

As the psychometric model described in Chapter 8 made clear, we should be able to predict educational success (as, indeed, any other behaviour) with a linear equation including the main ability, personality and motivational variables, together with some measurement of interactions with the environment. Cattell and Butcher (1968), in their study of creativity and educational achievement in 15-year-old children, did this, and their results showed that personality (the HSPQ) and motivation (the SMAT) contributed significantly and separately to the educational attainment variance. The multiple correlation overall with ability, personality and motivation was about 0.6, each of the separate categories having an overall correlation of about 0.25. Thus, the Cattell factors correlate to a small but significant extent with academic success, as the model predicts.

Prediction of academic achievement

The Cattell and Butcher (1968) study is just one of a huge number of investigations that have examined the link between personality and academic success. This research can be properly understood only in its context, since outside this framework the work seems almost senseless.

The *fons et origo* of the research into personality and educational achievement was the earlier, often applied research into the prediction of academic success using tests of intelligence and abilities. In Britain the now (unjustly) denigrated 11 + selection examination for grammar schools was the product of the application of this work. Intelligence-test scores show moderate correlations with academic achievement; if the whole range of ability is used, including ESN and lower levels, this correlation is substantially higher.

Two points were noted about this earlier research: first, the correlation was substantial; second, although it was substantial, much of the variance was left unexplained. This led to the introduction of personality tests as further predictive measures.

Kline (1977, 1979) has summarized much of this work which is simple to carry out, involves the correlation of personality test scores with examination marks and has formed the basis of many a thesis. However, its scientific value, unless followed up with further study, is slight.

Summary of results

At the primary school the extraverted, stable child (high E, high N) does best. Of the many studies showing this, a good one is that of Eysenck and Cookson (1969) because the sample was so large (4000). Correlations in both Britain and America are small, between 0.2 and 0.3, but significant in virtually all investigations. Although not too much should be made of these findings, for the correlations are small (96 per cent of the variance is unexplained), they make sense in the light of primary school teaching methods that encourage children to move from topic to topic and regard activities rather than quiet reading as the order of the day. Similarly, the finding that low N is associated with success is sensible, anxiety being regarded by educational psychologists as a major barrier to learning (e.g. Schonell, 1944).

These findings are confirmed using both the Eysenck factors and the Cattell second-orders. One of the claimed advantages of the Cattell test, as we saw in Chapter 3, is that the primaries yield more information than do the broader second-order factors. In fact, only factor G is of any value, with small but significant correlations with academic success (about 0.2). Thus the stable, extraverted, conscientious child tends to do slightly better at primary school – not a finding to shatter the educational world.   At the secondary level, the results are less clear-cut. In Britain the neurotic introvert performs best. However, these correlations are small – 0.2. The change from the primary pattern seems to occur at the fifth-form level (Warburton, 1968). This may be due to the emphasis at this stage on exam preparation and reading, activities which the stimulus-hungry extravert finds unrewarding.

Similar results are obtained with the Eysenck and Cattell tests, although, as Cattell and Kline (1977) noted, the primaries loading the Cattell extraversion factor do not behave in the same way: high F and Q2 are correlated with academic success, but low A. This suggests that the Cattell test may be more sensitive than the EPI and EPQ in this context.

However, in America the stable introvert performs best academically. Before this result can be interpreted it must be remembered that in other cultures in which secondary-school children have been subjects – for example, in Uganda (Honess and Kline, 1974a) and in India (Madan, 1967) – the results are similar to those obtained in Britain.

The sensible but *post hoc* explanation of these results is that the greater emphasis on book learning at the secondary-school level favours the introvert rather than the extravert, who is suited by primary school teaching methods. The success of the neurotic in countries other than the USA has been used as an example of the Yerkes–Dodson law – a curvilinear relationship between anxiety and performance. Thus the mildly neurotic individual worries over his performance, and if this is unsatisfactory, he strives to improve. The stable child remains unworried by his failures. All this is sound but for two counter-arguments. First, no such curvilinear relationship between N and academic success has ever been noted. Second, it fails to account for the discrepancy between American and other results. (This discrepancy has never been convincingly explained, and the present writer cannot account for it.) Finally, it must be remembered that these correlations are small and conclusions must be duly cautious.

In higher education the results are similar but not identical to those at the secondary level. In the USA almost all investigations show small but significant correlations between stability and introversion and academic success. In the USA, therefore, the picture is the same as at the secondary school. In Britain, however, the findings are slightly more complex. The introvert always does better, but the highest correlation, noted by Entwistle (1972) in his survey of the work, was only 0.26 (i.e. only just over 6 per cent of the variance is accounted for by introversion). Factor N is more equivocal. In some studies the correlation is small but positive, in others small but negative, in others non-significant. Entwistle tries to account for these results in terms of subject differences. The stable introvert excels at history and natural science, the neurotic introvert at engineering and languages. Kline and Gale (1971), incidentally, found no correlation between success at psychology and either E or N. This fits these claims, since psychology is a social science.

However, Entwistle's (1972) arguments simply will not do. The question remains of what precisely there is in common between engineering and languages, history and natural science. Certainly, an *a priori* analysis would not thus categorize these subjects.

Before concluding this section on the relation of personality traits to academic performance, two further points must be raised. First, at the higher education level – in India (Madan, 1967), in Uganda (Honess and Kline, 1974b) and in Ghana (Kline, 1966a) – the basic finding that neurotic introverts were academically successful held. Indeed, the highest correlation found in this field (about 0.6) emerged in the Ghanaian study. As far as the Ugandan and Ghanaian results were concerned, the results were not an artefact of the test's (the EPI) failure to work in these cultures, since item analyses demonstrated that the N and E scales were behaving as intended. We were surprised that in cultures manifestly as different from the British as those of Uganda and Ghana the same variables should influence academic success.

Finally, brief mention must be made of the fact that some of the other temperamental variables shown by us to be important in the description of personality, such as those of the DPI, have also been shown to have small correlations with academic success (e.g. Hamilton, 1970). These findings are difficult to interpret, since the validity of the individual scales of the DPI is highly dubious (Kline and Storey, 1978), although they clearly measure variance separate from that of the Eysenck and Cattell scales.

Conclusions　We have dealt with the topic of the relationship of academic success to personality variables at some length (a) because considerable research effort has been devoted to it and (b) because since there are correlations, they support the psychometric model of man and, *ipso facto*, provide evidence for the trait approach to personality and are one link in the argument against situationalism.

On the other hand, the correlations are small. Only about 1 per cent of educational variance is explained by these factors. Furthermore, as we have seen, the results are equivocal. What is needed is not further research with larger or more highly selected samples but more highly concentrated studies that attempt to account for the correlations – for example, studies of the behaviour of teachers and students measuring the interaction with personality-test scores. Then it might be found that certain methods and procedures enable pupils of given personality configurations to perform well and that these methods are employed most effectively by teachers of certain personality patterns. Studies of this kind could throw theoretical light on the processes of education, learning and teaching and might in practice enable pupils to be allocated to teachers who would be most effective for them. This would be rational educational research, gathering evidence with quantified measures and with the theoretical rationale of the psychometric model.

The motivational variables and academic success

There has been far less research into academic success using the motivational variables, and our discussion can be rather brief. In Cattell and Butcher's (1968) study with adolescents, to which we have already referred, the multiple correlation of the SMAT scales with performance was only 0.164. This means that as a predictor of school success it is not powerful. Indeed, the only point to be made in its favour is that its predictive power is separate from that of temperamental and ability variables – a finding which fits the psychometric model, of course.

However, more recent investigations, such as those of Barton and Cattell (Bartsch *et al.*, 1973; Cattell *et al.*, 1972), have analysed the integrated and unintegrated SMAT scores separately. They claim (as do Cattell and Child, 1975, who summarize these recent studies) that the good academic performer is high on total curiosity, integrated self-sentiment and super-ego but low on total pugnacity and narcissism and on integrated gregariousness.

Although these results make sound intuitive psychological sense, in that, for example, the gregarious person will have less time to spend on study than a solitary individual, it would be wrong to make too much of them. First, as the study by Cooper and Kline (1982) indicates, the

MAT items do not form the clear factors, at least in Britain, as intended by the authors of the test. Furthermore, as was the case with temperamental variables, the correlations with academic success are small, albeit significant. In respect of this, readers should be careful in their examination of Cattell and Child (1975), who argue that motivational variables account for 25 per cent of the educational achievement variance. This figure was obtained after the correlations had been corrected for the unreliability of both tests and criteria. The interpretation and meaning of such boosted figures is dubious.

In conclusion, then, the basic finding that motivational variables help to predict school achievement, as Cattell and Butcher (1968) originally found, is supported. However, their contribution to the prediction is marginal, and care must be taken not to exaggerate the practical importance of the findings.

Thus it can be seen that in accord with the psychometric model, dynamic and temperamental variables do predict academic performance. In practice, however, other determinants of academic success are more important, such as abilities and, presumably, the experience of the child in home and school.

Clinical assessment

We have discussed the prediction of academic achievement based on using tests in assessments in some detail because a considerable amount of research has been undertaken in this field, and the results fall into some kind of order.

However, the comparable work in the clinical field belongs more properly to our category of diagnosis and treatment; tests have been used to examine differences between different kinds of mentally disturbed patient and between psychiatric cases and normals.

Assessment in occupational psychology

This is an area in which tests have been extensively used mainly for selection but also for guidance and counselling. We shall restrict our discussion in this section to the use of personality tests for occupational selection. Their use in guidance and counselling is discussed in a later section of this chapter.

As is implied in the psychometric model (see Chapter 8), one approach to this problem is to correlate trait scores with job success and to obtain the beta weights and the multiple correlations. This then indicates the extent of the predictive power of the tests and the most important variables. A different line of attack is to compare the mean scores of different occupational groups on the personality factors or, better, the whole profile of scores. If there is any force in the psychometric model, scores of different occupational groups should differ, since to some extent dynamics and temperament must influence occupational choice. We shall first discuss the results of this second approach.

Temperamental and dynamic differences between occupational groups

Most of the relevant research in this field has been conducted by Cattell and his colleagues at Illinois. Much of this information, and certainly that on which we are basing the present account, is contained in two publications: Cattell and Child (1975) for the dynamic factors and Cattell *et al.* (1970a), the technical handbook for the 16PF test, for the temperamental factors. We have examined this work in great detail previously (Kline, 1979), and we shall here summarize the conclusions that may be drawn from it.

Table 2 shows the mean differences on the 16PF and MAT factors for a number of occupational groups. These are only a selection from the two main sources, but they have been chosen because they illustrate well the strengths and weaknesses of this method.

In examining this table, the mean differences on individual factors between the groups are clearly of interest. Cattell *et al.* (1970a), however, argue that of even more psychological significance are the differences between the whole profiles of scores for which special statistics have been developed, since few can make large numbers of simultaneous comparisons in their heads. It must also be borne in mind when scrutinizing these results that these figures are stens (i.e. they have means of 5.5 and standard deviations of 1.5). Finally, it must also be realized that the value of these figures depends on the adequacy of the sampling of the various occupations. The samples should be both representative and large. This is not always the case with these samples, so care has to be taken in interpreting the results. Nevertheless, some data, however imperfect, are better than no data.

To what extent these occupational profiles make psychological sense and fit the psychometric model – thus refuting situationalism

Table 2 *Personality and motivational variables and occupation*

Sphere	Occupation Army officers (or cadets)	Executives	Air pilots	Artists	Theology students	Physicians	Physicists	Engineers	Teachers	Writers
Personality sphere										
A	5.4	7.8	5.1	3.1	5.9	5.4	2.9	5.9	5.6	4.1
B	6.0	7.5	7.2	8.8	6.6	6.2	9.6	6.3	6.5	9.7
C	6.1	5.7	7.8	7.7	6.5	5.4	7.3	4.3	5.0	6.6
E	5.6	5.8	6.0	6.8	5.7	4.8	6.2	5.3	5.5	8.1
F	5.9	5.3	6.7	3.4	5.8	5.6	3.1	1.6	5.5	4.6
G	6.4	5.5	7.2	3.7	5.2	5.1	3.9	4.8	5.7	3.2
H	5.7	6.6	6.9	7.0	5.8	5.4	6.1	4.4	5.6	7.0
I	5.0	5.6	3.8	9.2	6.8	5.7	6.8	5.4	5.9	7.9
L	5.2	5.4	3.7	5.0	4.7	5.4	3.8	6.4	5.0	5.3
M	5.4	5.7	4.1	8.9	5.7	5.5	4.8	6.8	5.4	7.3
N	6.1	6.2	5.7	4.4	4.3	5.8	5.6	5.3	5.8	5.1
O	4.6	5.5	3.5	4.8	4.6	5.5	3.7	6.3	5.1	5.4
Q_1	5.5	6.4	5.8	6.4	4.9	5.6	5.6	6.8	5.5	6.9
Q_2	5.4	5.5	5.1	7.0	5.3	6.4	6.3	7.0	5.7	7.2
Q_3	6.3	5.6	7.5	6.3	5.4	6.1	7.2	6.4	6.0	5.9
Q_4	5.2	5.3	3.0	6.3	5.8	5.0	5.1	6.7	5.3	6.7
Dynamic sphere										
Career	6	6			5	6		7	5	
Home	4	3			4	3		5	3	
Fear	5	5			4	6		5	5	
Narcissism	8	10			6	8		5	3	
Super-ego	4	1			6	6		5	5	
Self-sentiment	5	10			6	7		5	7	
Mating	6	8			5	5		5	6	
Pugnacity	7	4			5	6		5	5	
Assertion	5	5			4	5		6	5	
Sweetheart	6	6			6	4		6	6	

Reprinted by kind permission of Academic Press from P. Kline, *Psychometrics and psychology* (1979).

and the opponents of trait psychology – must now be discussed. In our view, they do support the psychometric model and thus are useful for selection for the following reasons.

Some of the observed differences between groups make sound psychological sense. For example, accountants score high on B intelligence and A sociability. On other factors accountants resemble the general population. This suggests that the accountant is an anonymous, grey figure of no great distinction. His sociability is probably useful, in that he gets on well with his clients. As we have argued previously (Kline, 1979), an adventurous, unconventional (H+, M+) accountant could be a menace. However, although the accountants' scores make good sense, the personality factors are not sufficiently discriminating to allow the test to be used on its own for selection.

Again, with the profile for air pilots the results are sensible. The air pilots are high on C (ego strength), G (conscientiousness) and Q_3 (will-power); they are low on L (projection), O (guilt proneness) and Q_4 (tension). One would perhaps travel with more confidence than if the results were reversed. Finally, it is worth comparing the scores of artists, writers and physicists. These three groups have about half of their scores on the 16PF test at least a standard deviation away from the mean. If these factor scores account in any way for their success, this finding would explain the relative rarity of such persons in the population: by statistical definition few such individuals could occur. This means that while it might be easy to increase the flow of accountants (heaven forfend), this would not be so easy for these more creative groups. The factors by which these groups were distinguished again make sound intuitive sense. Artists are Bohemian and tender-minded; physicists are withdrawn and of high ego strength. Again, therefore, it is possible to argue that these trait differences among occupational groups support the psychometric model. On the other hand, they are not large enough to make accurate selection possible on their basis.

Before drawing conclusions about these results, we shall consider the first approach, that by which multiple correlations and beta weights are calculated between the factor scores and occupational criteria. In fact, there are far fewer such studies than those comparing mean scores. This is partly because of the problem of obtaining adequate measures of occupational success. Indeed, it is probably fair to argue that there is no agreed criterion for such success. The best procedure is probably to regress the factor scores on to each criterion separately (e.g. money earned, supervisor's ratings).

There is a further difficulty with the multiple regression approach which applies to other multivariate procedures, such as discriminant factions or canonical analyses. To be reliable the beta weights need to be obtained from large samples – at least 200 subjects are usually recommended (e.g. Nunnally, 1978). With smaller samples replication is essential; without this, the interpretation of results has to be duly cautious. Unfortunately, few of the studies quoted in Cattell *et al.* (1970a) met these stringent but necessary criteria.

These studies are superior to those discussed in connection with the first approach because by regressing the factors on to success in the job, one actually knows that factors with high beta weights are involved in such success. Using the first method, the high or low scores might be irrelevant to success at the particular job. The results, however, while promising (for example, low A and F and L were important for successful patrolmen and A, H and Q₂ for good salesmen), are still not sufficiently clear-cut to allow such beta weights to be used for selection on their own. Clearly, they are useful in a regression equation with variables from other domains, but even so prediction would be far from perfect.

Conclusions concerning the use of the temperamental factors for selection for jobs

1　The differences on personality traits between occupational groups are not so great that these tests would be used on their own for selection purposes without considerable error.
2　However, differences are such that trait scores would be likely to improve selection procedures by other methods.
3　The results do fit a psychometric trait model of personality and accord well with psychological sense.
4　Personality traits do seem to be a determinant, albeit small, of occupational choice and success.

Results with motivational variables

As we saw in our chapter on tests of motivation, Cattell and his colleagues are the only workers who have submitted the field of motivation to factor analysis in order to establish its fundamental dimensions. Other workers have used *a priori* dimensions such as the needs of Murray (1938), notably Edwards and Jackson, but there is no reason other than personal predilection to choose these in preference to others. The majority of workers have used interest tests (e.g. Strong), which simply measure interests as categorized in everyday life. Our rationale demands that only factorially identified dimensions merit study as a basis for theoretical analysis, so we shall examine here only those results derived from the MAT. Its school version (the SMAT) has not been used in studies of occupational selection.

Most of these results are summarized in Cattell and Child (1975), the source for Table 2. In fact, far fewer studies have been conducted than is the case with the 16PF test, and great care has to be taken not to exaggerate the significance of the results, since the samples are not large for most of the studies and also because the validity and meaning of the MAT scales are not well established.

As was the case with the temperamental scales, the results are modest support for the psychometric model in that many of the mean differences between occupational groups make good sense but in general the results are still not sufficiently clear-cut to make the MAT powerful on its own for job selection. Since its variance is distinct from that of temperament and ability, it would probably be useful to add it to a selection battery.

There is no doubt that some of these factor differences are striking. For example, narcissism is high in executives, low in teachers. It is hard to imagine a narcissistic teacher surviving in a tough school. Readers can see other similar examples in Table 2. There is, however, no clear discrimination between these groups.

Conclusions   It is obvious that on both temperamental and dynamic factors there is too much overlap between the various occupational groups for clear selection to be possible: it cannot be claimed, for example, that any subjects with a given set of scores should automatically be selected for any particular job. Nor are the multiple correlations with job success high enough to produce a specification equation for any job that could be followed with confidence. However, modest discriminations can be obtained, and these temperamental and dynamic factors could play a useful part in a selection battery. Finally, even these modest correlations do support the psychometric trait model of personality.

Diagnosis and treatment

Diagnosis and treatment are aspects mainly of educational and clinical psychology, and at this point these two applied fields are essentially so similar that they can be treated together in respect of the contribution to be expected from tests of personality and motivation.

We have previously argued that factored tests reveal fundamental dimensions, whereas criterion-keyed tests merely allow for discrimination between criterion groups, and such scales do not necessarily have psychological implications. This is important in the use of psychometric personality and motivation tests for diagnosis and treatment because factored tests, since they have psychological meaning, can provide us with useful psychological insight into these problems, which merely discriminatory tests are unable to do. For this reason we shall concentrate on the results with factor-analytic scales.

The relevant results, the scores of neurotic and psychotic groups, on the 16PF test and EPQ and EPI tests (for these are the most deeply researched factors) can be found in the handbook to these tests. Fortunately, it is possible to summarize the findings with some clarity.

1　Compared with normals, the neurotic patient has low ego strength (C−), is submissive (E−), is sober and taciturn (F), of low super-ego strength (G−), timid (H−) and anxious and guilty (O, Q_4). This picture confirms the typical delineation of a neurotic patient (e.g. Mayer-Gross *et al.*, 1967), and in part it supports the psychoanalytic claims that neurotics have poor egos. However, it does not fit with the high super-ego that psychoanalysis claims to be important in neurosis.

2　The neurotic patient tends (second-order factors) to be an anxious introvert.

3　Although neurotics are discriminated from normals in terms of normal dimensions of personality, psychotic groups such as schizophrenics are not so discriminated. These are discriminated by abnormal factors, of which measures were specially developed by Cattell and colleagues (Delhees and Cattell, 1971).

4　These special abnormal factors (seven depressive factors plus paranoia, psychopathy, schizophrenia, psyasthenia and psychosis) discriminate the main psychotic and neurotic groups from normals.

5　Thus neurotics differ from normals on both normal and abnormal factors. Psychotics differ from normals on the abnormal factors only.

6　There are two implications of these findings: (a) psychosis, neurosis and mental health do not lie on a continuum, hence psychosis is qualitatively different from mental health and neurosis; (b) neurosis is on a continuum with mental health, and some symptoms can be regarded as an exaggeration of normal personality traits, so an important insight into the nature of mental illness can be gained from the application of factored personality tests to diagnosis and treatment.

As is clear from a perusal of Cattell and Child (1975), there is simply insufficient work with the MAT on clinical samples of sufficient size to warrant any conclusions to be drawn. In this area, the research needs to be carried out, although it is likely that interesting differences in ergic patterns could be obtained in the comparison of normal and psychotic groups.

As regards diagnosis in problem children, there is as yet little work with factored variables, although in principle the methods described above in the context of the study of clinical patients are applicable. It is to be expected that meaningful differences between children differentially classified would throw light on the nature of the mental disturbance.

In respect of treatment there is surprisingly little reported research (for summaries, see Cattell and Kline, 1977), so that our brief discussion here will be concerned with how psychometric personality and motivation tests might most profitably be used. It is generally agreed that the measurement of the effects of therapy is exceedingly difficult. As Kiesler (1966) pointed out, in any group of neurotic patients there are considerable individual differences among the patients. Similarly, among therapists, even of a given school or orientation, there are large individual differences. In addition, a further problem in the study of therapeutic efficiency is the establishment of a good criterion for recovery. In our view, the proper use of psychometric tests can help to resolve these problems and can play a part in actually measuring therapeutic outcome. This can be achieved as briefly summarized below.

1 Patients should be given the tests containing the major personality and motivation factors at the onset of treatment and at intervals throughout the treatment. In this way changes in the pattern of scores can be monitored.
2 Therapists should take these tests. Thus the personality pattern of therapists can be utilized in the investigations.
3 These personality tests allow a rational measure of therapeutic

success. Thus, as we pointed out in our section on diagnosis, neurotics and psychotics can be discriminated from normals by scores on certain factors. Effective treatment should, therefore, return these elevated scores to normal. Notice that this does not mean that treatment should make patients just like everybody else and rob them of their individuality. It should leave untouched scores on variables unconnected with mental illness. Treatment should change simply the critical factors.

This approach not only permits the objective and rational measurement of improvement but it also allows the investigator to measure the interaction of the personality of the patient, the personality of the therapist, the type of therapy used and its effects on improvement. So far little research of this kind has been done, although Cattell (1980) has advocated this approach under the heading of depth psychometrics.

Any results should be useful both practically, because they might well suggest what kinds of patient (in terms of category of disturbance and pattern of personality) is likely to prove successful with what kind of therapist and therapy, and theoretically, because any findings will require some theoretical account.

From this it can be concluded that the psychometry of personality could play a valuable part in treatment and diagnosis.

Before leaving this topic of diagnosis and treatment two further points can be made. The first concerns objective tests. In principle, the use of objective tests in this context is no different from the use of questionnaire measures. Indeed, in the light of the problems of their reliability and validity (fully discussed in Chapter 1) it would appear premature to so employ them. However, a study by Cattell *et al.*, (1972) deserves mention; in this the battery of objective tests, measuring the most important T factors, was administered to 114 subjects on two occasions, these subjects including all the main categories of mental patient. Discriminant functions showed that normals could be discriminated from neurotics with considerable clarity. Furthermore, powerful discrimination among these groups was also obtained – 75 per cent of cases were correctly classified. When state factors were included, this figure rose to 98 per cent.

If these results were replicable with other groups in further studies, despite the problems with the proper identification of T (objective) factors, this in itself would be a notable diagnostic achievement. Its theoretical implication, given the nature of factors, would also be considerable.

The other technique that has proved useful in clinical psychology is G analysis, especially of projective tests, and we shall summarize some of the findings that have been obtained from it. As we described in our chapter on projective tests, G analysis (Holley, 1973) involved the objective scoring of projective tests using dichotomous scores (0 or 1), the correlation of subjects rather than scores, using G indices, and the Q factoring of these G indices. By this method subjects were classified into groups. This procedure is obviously useful for research into diagnosis.

Holley (1973) described his G analyses of the Rorschach test. In three studies, schizophrenics, normals and depressives were categorized with an extremely high degree of accuracy. This, of course, implies that the Rorschach test (*pace* Eysenck) is a useful diagnostic tool, that G analysis is a powerful diagnostic technique and that the standard Kraepelinian categories are meaningful. These results were *a priori* unlikely, but Holley and colleagues have confirmed them with further studies in Lund.

Hampson and Kline (1977) used G analysis with samples of criminals, petty offenders and murderers and the HTP and CAT tests, among others. Although some interesting discriminations within the offender groups were made, a problem arose concerning the identification of the factors, which ultimately is inevitably subjective. It was by no means clear in some instances whether the factors discriminating the groups in different samples were the same or not. On the other hand, among some Broadmoor murderers a clear distinction between the over- and under-controlled type seemed to emerge. This study confirmed the value of G analysis in the study of groups.

Further studies using G analysis have been carried out by Jonsson (1975) with schizophrenics, from which four categories emerged; by Holley and Nilsson (1973), in which a highly disturbed and a less disturbed group were found; and by Jonsson and Franzen (1976), from which clear groups emerged, although the relevant factors were not as clear-cut. Finally, to conclude our examples from the Lund and Uppsala laboratories, Fallstrom and Vegelius (1976) used an elaborated form of G analysis of Rorschach data in the study of diabetic children, work replicated by Vegelius (1976). In each case there was virtually perfect discrimination of diabetic and non-diabetic children.

Finally, two papers summarizing work on clinical diagnosis at the Max Planck Institute (Schubo *et al.*, 1975, and Hentschel *et al.*,

1976) report research in which symptom questionnaires were given to 454 patients (depressives, neurotics and psychotics, schizophrenics and paranoids). Various methods of categorizing these patients were used – discriminant functions and scores in the two scales, as well as G analysis. This last produced the highest number of correct placements: 83 per cent.

Conclusions As yet G analysis and its related methods (see Vegelius, 1976) have not produced substantive psychological knowledge. However, there is no doubt that it is a powerful technique in the study of diagnosis. It would be equally suitable for the investigation of successful and unsuccessful treatments for mental disorders.

Vocational guidance and counselling

Most of the findings relevant to occupational selection (discussed above) are, of course, relevant to vocational guidance and counselling. Here, indeed, the results could be even more useful, since their lack of precise prediction, the fact that they give general indications rather than exact information, is an advantage for the findings can be used as a basis for discussion.

We have suggested elsewhere that further research into the predictions of job success and into the differences between occupational groups could lead to the gradual writing of an encyclopaedia of job specifications in terms of the major factored variables (Kline, 1979). Thus, the vocational counsellor, having obtained his client's pattern of test scores, could look up this pattern in the encyclopaedia to find the jobs most closely related to the pattern. These could then be discussed with the client. At present, since predictions are far from perfect, to temper the results with sensitive discussion makes good sense. This basis for discussion would be factual and would compare well with many of the intuitive hunches used at present in vocational guidance, hunches perhaps inevitable in the absence of factual knowledge.

Theory

Finally, we come to the contribution to clinical theory made by psychometric personality tests. At present, there is little to write about, since the collection of the data has only just begun. Nevertheless, both Eysenck and Cattell have adumbrated theoretical accounts, and these will be briefly discussed. Eysenck's theoretical position has been fully discussed in Chapter 9. As applied to clinical psychology, the learning theoretic account of abnormal behaviour postulates that it arises from maladaptive learning. Symptoms are learned responses due to conditioning, which is, of course, influenced by a subject's position on E and N. In essence, therefore, treatment consists of extinguishing the maladaptive responses and conditioning more appropriate ones. Precisely how this is done is the subject matter of behaviour therapy. Furthermore, status on the newer factor, P, is claimed to affect the likelihood of behaviour-therapeutic success (Eysenck and Eysenck, 1976).

Unfortunately, this simple and elegant account does not entirely fit clinical experience, so Eysenck (1976) has been forced to modify this aspect of his theorizing with what he calls 'incubation theory'. This addendum deals with the fact that while insect and snake phobias are relatively common, most patients, in Britain at least, have never had unpleasant experiences with the creatures. On the other hand, electric plug or gas tap phobias are rare, although these are devices with which many people have had extremely unpleasant experiences. The explanation in incubation theory is that human beings are genetically programmed to be especially reactive to some stimuli rather than others (snakes, not plugs). Further, the rarity of reinforcement or its absence does not lead to the extinction of these responses; rather, the opposite occurs. This, of course, leads to the position that both reinforcement and non-reinforcement can lead to the same symptoms. While this may be true, it must be pointed out that it is this very aspect of psychoanalytic theory (as embodied in reaction formation) that Eysenck has so strenuously objected to in the past (e.g. 1957).

In conclusion, impressive as is Eysenck's attempt to account for clinical observations within his theoretical framework, it must be argued that it is not entirely successful. Both the theory itself and the account it can yield of clinical findings are imperfect.

In Chapter 9 we also discussed Cattell's structural learning theory and his attempt to weave into it the results of his studies of motivation, the ergs and sentiments. We have also, in this chapter and elsewhere, discussed his specification equations.

Here we shall examine the relevance of this theorizing to clinical psychology. As yet, there is not much research that bears on clinical theory, and Cattell and Child's (1975) attempt to develop a dynamic calculus to account for the integrative action of the ergs, and the even more recent VIDAS model, are mathematically complex and quite speculative without the support of data. Here we shall suggest some simpler contributions to clinical theorizing that could easily be put into operation and do not involve as yet unworked mathematical approaches and measurement techniques (as does, for example, the VIDAS model) or the measurement of the environment in the dynamic calculus.

The simple approach which could lead to useful gains in clinical theory is the application of P-factor analysis, the analysis of repeated measures from a subject. For example, in a study by Kline and Grindley (1974) that has already been mentioned, the MAT was administered every day and related to diary events over a period of a month. These were the basic data for P analysis. Let us take some clinical examples.

1 Obsessional neurosis. Administer the MAT at regular intervals to measure ergs and sentiments. Note all obsessional behaviours – hand washing, wall touching, anxiety-provoking thoughts and other symptoms. P-factor analysis over the occasions will reveal the tension-reducing and tension-assessing nature of these behaviours. Such a study could well answer much of the clinical theorizing about the nature of obsessionality. As this example demonstrates, P analysis is peculiarly suited to the study of dynamics. Thus dynamic theory is where it is most telling.

2 If we measure regularly the musical, artistic and literary achievements of creative people, together with ergic and temperamental measures, P analysis can again reveal the dynamics of such activity, if any.

Studies of clinical therapeutic sessions in which patient and therapist behaviours, together with trait and dynamic measures and outcome measures, could also help to answer many theoretical questions concerning the mechanism of therapy.

Thus this basic factor-analytic approach utilizing the methods and procedures advocated by Cattell could, in our view, make a valuable contribution to clinical theory. Indeed, the research outlined above would, in fact, enable one to construct the dynamic lattice showing the dynamics of behaviour, a Cattellian concept which at present is founded on speculation.

Summary

1 The boundaries and definitions of clinical, educational and occupational psychology were identified.

2 Four categories of problems, by no means entirely separate, were recognized as common to all three branches of applied psychology. The main contributions of the psychometric approaches to these problems were then described and examined.

3 The following areas were scrutinized:

(a) Assessment in education: the prediction of academic success by tests of personality and motivation; the varying influence of extraversion and neuroticism; the need for more detailed studies of learning behaviour to account for the results.

(b) Assessment in occupational groups: the prediction of job success and the discrimination of the occupants of different jobs by personality and motivation tests.

(c) Clinical diagnosis and treatment:

(i) the differences between clinical and normal groups and among clinical groups were described. Their implications for diagnosis and treatment were then discussed.

(ii) the use of G analysis with projective tests was considered a useful research technique.

(iii) objective (T) results from clinical studies were also described.

(d) The use of these tests in vocational guidance and counselling was outlined.

(e) The bearing of the results on clinical theory was discussed. P-factor analyses were advocated.

12 Conclusions

In this final chapter we shall summarize, under separate headings, the argument proposed in this book and its inevitable conclusions. In our view, this theme is no longer understood in modern psychology, and its demise accounts for the attacks on psychometrics and its subsequent neglect. This, as is obvious from this book, is a severe loss for the scientific study of personality.

1 Various problems associated with the construction of psychological tests were scrutinized and the characteristics of good tests were defined: high validity, high reliability in most circumstances, high discriminatory power and good norms unless special scaling methods, such as Rasch scaling, were used.

2 Different methods of measuring personality were then examined against these criteria of good tests. It was concluded that among these methods only personality tests could be regarded as even adequate measuring instruments. The various types of personality test were then discussed and scrutinized.

3 Two types of personality questionnaire were identified: those constructed by criterion-keying, such as the MMPI, and those constructed by factor analysis or analogous techniques. It was shown that only the latter variety had any psychological meaning and were thus to be preferred. This meaning was further shown to derive from the nature of factor analysis itself – its ability to uncover fundamental dimensions underlying observed correlations.

4 Projective tests were described and discussed. It was shown that many of the objections to such tests raised by academic psychologists on grounds of reliability and validity could be countered by objective marking schemes and careful multivariate analysis, notably G analysis. It was concluded that, thus used, projective tests could yield valuable information in the field of personality.

5 Objective tests were examined and found to be, of all tests,

probably the most potentially useful. However, at present, it was clear that there was a desperate need for research into their validity.

6 Having covered the main types of temperament test, we then examined measures of personality dynamics – moods and states. Moods and states were defined as transient by contrast with the more enduring traits. State- and trait-change factors were then described. Motivation tests were examined and factor-analytic methods were shown to yield the most useful results. A number of ergs and sentiments were described, together with some strength-of-motivation factors.

7 From this scrutiny of tests, and given the ability of factor analysis to reveal the fundamental variables of a field, it was argued that the best established factor-analytic tests of temperament, dynamic and mood, would yield the variables that should be incorporated into any adequate theory of personality. The most important variables in the field were then described – extraversion, anxiety, psychoticism, tender-mindedness, radicalism, obsessionality – together with certain dynamic factors. Such a list was not regarded as fixed or final; it was suggested that it would be modified in the light of research.

8 A psychometric model of man incorporating all these variables was then described, a linear specification equation for any behaviour, for which the weights would be determined by empirical investigation. It was shown that such a model is a variant of a trait model, and the fact that data can be fitted to it was used as an argument in the refutation of situationalism.

9 The psychometric model is a general model: any variables can be inserted into it. However, two more specific theories of personality were described and scrutinized, those of Eysenck and Cattell, which use specific sets of factorially defined variables and constitute attempts to base personality theories on the factor-analytic results. Eysenck's conditioning model, using psychophysiological components, was found wanting in certain respects, while Cattell's structured learning theory and the more recent VIDAS model were found to be far in advance of the objective evidence. Such theorizing, however, with its factor-analytic basis, is clearly what needs to be done.

10 The bearing of the factored results on clinical theories of personality, psychoanalytic, personological and others, was then examined. It was shown that certain aspects of these theories

were supported by the evidence, although much of the detail did not appear to be accurate.

11 The relevance and impact of the factored work in educational, occupational and clinical psychology were then assessed. It was demonstrated that, as the psychometric model predicts, these tests are highly useful in selection and guidance. In addition, it was shown how powerful such personality tests could be in formulating clinical theory as it relates to effective psychotherapy.

From all these points a few simple conclusions can be drawn. Although these conclusions are simple, their implications are considerable, and they could put the study of personality firmly back into the sphere of science.

12 It is essential that further factor-analytic work be carried out in all the relevant fields – temperament, dynamics and mood – so that the major factors can be properly identified. This should be done not only with questionnaires but also with objective tests, which potentially are the most valuable.

13 Experimental studies should be carried out aimed at identifying the psychological nature of these factors, determining their correlates and the kinds of subjects who score high or low on them.

14 Clinical and occupational groups of every kind should be given these factored tests so that specification equations and group differentiations could be determined. All this research would yield highly valuable insights in these fields.

15 These new data would then form a truly sound base on which to develop theories of personality which could be quantitatively tested.

These are the true objects of the psychometric approach to personality. The future is clear. It remains only to carry out the research.

Bibliography

Abraham, K. (1921), 'Contribution to the theory of the anal character', in *Selected Papers of Karl Abraham* (1965), London: Hogarth Press and Institute of Psychoanalysis

Adorno, T. W., Frenkel-Brunswick, E., Levinson, D. J., and Sanford, R. N. (1950), *The Authoritarian Personality*, New York: Harper

Allport, G. W., and Vernon, P. E. (1933), *Studies in Expressive Movement*, New York: Macmillan

Anastasi, A. (1972), 'The personality research form', in Buros (1972)

Andrich, D., and Kline, P. (1981), 'Within and among population item fit with the simple logistic model', *Educ. Psychol. Meas.* (in press)

Appley, M. H., and Trumbull, R. (eds.) (1967), *Psychological Stress: Issues in Research*, New York: Appleton-Century-Crofts

Bannister, D., and Mair, J. M. M. (1968), *The Evaluation of Personal Constructs*, London: Academic Press

Barrett, P., and Kline, P. (1980), 'Personality factors in the EPQ', *Person. and Indiv. Diffs.*, **1**, 317–23

Barrett, P., and Kline, P. (1981a), 'The itemetric properties of the EPQ: a reply to Helmes', *Appl. Psychol. Meas.* (in press)

Barrett, P., and Kline, P. (1981b), 'Factor extraction: an examination of three methods', *Personality Study and Group Behaviour* (in press)

Barrett, P., and Kline, P. (1982), 'The Structure of the 16PF test by item and parcel factor analysis', *Person. and Indiv. Diffs.* (in press)

Barton, K. (1973), quoted by Cattell (1973)

Bartsch, T., Barton, K., and Cattell, R. B. (1973), 'A repeated measures investigation of the relations of the school Motivation Analysis Test to academic achievement', *Psychol. Rep.*, **33**, 743–8

Beck, S. J. (1952), *Rorschach's Test*, vol. 3: *Advances in Interpretation*, New York: Grune & Stratton

Bellak, L., Bellak, S. S., and Haworth, M. R. (1974), *Children's Apperception Test*, CPS Larchmont

Bendig, A. W. (1959), 'Score reliability of dichotomous and trichotomous item responses in the MPI', *J. Consult. Psychol.*, **23**, 181–5

Block, J. (1977), 'Advancing the psychology of personality. Paradigmatic shift or improving the quality of research', in Magnussen and Endler (1977)

Blum, G. S. (1949), 'A study of the psychoanalytic theory of psychosexual development', *Genet. Psychol. Monogr.*, **39**, 3–99

Boden, M. (1977), *Artificial Intelligence and Natural Man*, Hassocks: Harvester Press

Brand, C. (1980), personal communication

Briggs, K. C., and Myers, I. B. (1962), *The Myers–Briggs Type Indicator* (Manual), ETS Princeton

Broadhurst, P. L. (1960), 'Application of biometrical genetics to the inheritance of behaviour', in H. J. Eysenck (ed.), *Experiments in Personality*, vol. 1: *Psychogenetics and Psychopharmacology*, London: Routledge & Kegan Paul

Brown, R. (1965), *Social Psychology*, New York: Free Press

Browne, J. A., and Howarth, E. (1977), 'A comprehensive factor analysis of personality questionnaire items: a test of 20 putative factor hypotheses', *Multiv. Behav. Res.*, **12**, 399–427

Buck, J. N. (1948), 'The HTP test', *J. Clin. Psychol.*, **4**, 151–9

Buck, J. N. (1970), *The House Tree Person Technique: Revised Manual*, Los Angeles: WPS

Burdsall, C. (1975), 'An examination of second-order motivational factors as found in adults', *J. Genetic. Psychol.*, **125**, 83–90

Buros, O. K. (ed.) (1959), *The V Mental Measurement Year Book*, New Jersey: Gryphon Press

Buros, O. K. (ed.) (1972), *The VII Mental Measurement Year Book*, New Jersey: Gryphon Press

Buros, O. K. (ed.) (1978), *The VIII Mental Measurement Year Book*, New Jersey: Gryphon Press

Cattell, R. B. (1946), *Description and Measurement of Personality*, London: Harrap

Cattell, R. B. (1957), *Personality and Motivation Structure and Measurement*, Yonkers, NY: New World Publishers

Cattell, R. B. (1965), *The Scientific Analysis of Personality*, Harmondsworth: Penguin

Cattell, R. B. (1966), 'The scree test for the number of factors', *Multiv. Behav. Res.*, **1**, 140–61

Cattell, R. B. (ed.) (1971a), *Handbook of Modern Personality Theory*, Champaign: University of Illinois Press

Cattell, R. B. (1971b), *Abilities, their Structure, Growth and Action*, New York: Houghton-Mifflin

Cattell, R. B. (1972), 'The 16PF and basic personality structure: a reply to Eysenck', *J. Behav. Sci.*, **1**, 169–87

Cattell, R. B. (1973), *Personality and Mood by Questionnaire*, New York: Jossey-Bass

Cattell, R. B. (1978), *The Scientific Use of Factor Analysis*, New York: Plenum Press

Cattell, R. B. (1980), *Personality and Learning Theory*, New York: Springer

Cattell, R. B., and Butcher, H. J. (1968), *The Prediction of Achievement and Creativity*, New York: Bobbs-Merrill

Cattell, R. B., and Child, D. (1975), *Motivation and Dynamic Structure*, London: Holt, Rinehart & Winston

Cattell, R. B., and Eber, H. W. (1954), *The IPAT Music Preference Test of Personality*, Champaign: IPAT

Cattell, R. B., and Gibbons, B. D. (1968), 'Personality structure of the combined Guilford and Cattell personality questionnaires', *J. Pers. Soc. Psychol.*, **9**, 107–20

Cattell, R. B., and Kline, P. (1977), *The Scientific Analysis of Personality and Motivation*, London: Academic Press

Cattell, R. B., and Luborsky, L. (1952), *The IPAT Humour Test of Personality*, Champaign: IPAT

Cattell, R. B., and Schuerger, J. M. (1978), *Personality Theory in Action: The Objective-Analytic Test Battery*, Champaign: IPAT

Cattell, R. B., and Warburton, F. W. (1965), *Objective Personality and Motivation Tests*, Champaign: University of Illinois Press

Cattell, R. B., Barton, K., and Dielman, T. E. (1972), 'Prediction of school achievement from motivation, personality and ability measures', *Psychol. Reports*, **30**, 35–43

Cattell, R. B., Eber, H. L., and Tatsuoka, M. M. (1970a), *The 16PF Test*, Champaign: IPAT

Cattell, R. B., Horn, J. L., and Sweney, A. B. (1970b), *Motivation Analysis Test*, Champaign: IPAT

Cattell, R. B., Schmidt, L. R., and Bjerstedt, A. (1972), 'Clinical diagnosis by the Objective Analytic Test Batteries', *Clin. Psychol. Monogr.*, 3411–78

Chamove, A. S., Eysenck, H. J., and Harlow, H. F. (1972), 'Personality in monkeys: factor analysis of rhesus social behaviour', *Q. J. Exp. Psychol.*, **24**, 496–504

Chopin, B. H. (1976), 'Recent developments in item banking: a review', in D. N. M. de Gruijter and L. J. T. Van der Kamp (eds.), *Advances in Educational and Psychological Measurement*, New York: Wiley

Clyde, D. J. (1960), 'Rating scales, behaviour inventories and drugs', in L. Uhr and J. Miller (eds.), *Drugs and Behavior*, New York: Wiley

Clyde, D. J. (1963), *Clyde Mood Scale*, Miami: University of Miami

Comrey, A. L. (1970), *The Comrey Personality Scales*, San Diego: Educational and Industrial Testing Service

Cooper, C., and Kline, P. (1980), 'The validity of the MAT', *Brit. J. Educ. Psychol.* (in press)

Corman, L. (1967), *Le Gribouillis*, Paris: Presses Universitaires de France

Corman, L. (1969), *Le test P.N. manuel*, Paris: Presses Universitaires de France

Cronbach, L. J. (1946), 'Response sets and test validity', *Educ. Psychol. Meas.*, **6**, 475–94

Cronbach, L. J. (1950), 'Further evidence on response sets and test design', *Educ. Psychol. Meas.,* **10**, 3–31

Cronbach, L. J. (1951), 'Coefficient Alpha and the internal structure of tests', *Psychom.,* **16**, 297–334

Cronbach, L. J. (1970), *Essentials of Psychological Testing*, New York: Harper & Row

Cronbach, L. J., and Meehl, P. E. (1955), 'Construct validity in psychological tests', *Psychol. Bull.,* **52**, 177–94

Curran, J. P., and Cattell, R. B. (1974), *The Eight-State Questionnaire*, Champaign: IPAT

Dahlstrom, E. G., and Welsh, G. S. (1960), *An MMPI Handbook*, London: Oxford University Press

De Gruitjer, D. N. M., and Van der Kamp, L. J. T. (eds.) (1976), *Advances in Psychological and Educational Measurement*, Chichester: Wiley

Delhees, K. H., and Cattell, R. B. (1971), 'The dimensions of pathology: proof of their projection beyond the normal 16PF source traits', *Person.,* **2**, 149–71

Edwards, A. L. (1957), *The Social Desirability Variable in Personality Research*, New York: Dryden

Edwards, A. L. (1959), *The Edwards Personal Preference Schedule*, New York: Psychological Corporation

Edwards, A. L. (1970), *The Edwards Personal Preference Schedule* (revised), New York: Psychological Corporation

Entwistle, N. J. (1972), 'Personality and academic attainment', *Brit. J. Educ. Psychol.,* **42**, 137–51

Epstein, S. (1977), 'Traits are alive and well', in Magnussen and Endler (1977)

Eysenck, H. J. (1947), *Dimensions of Personality*, London: Routledge & Kegan Paul

Eysenck, H. J. (1954), *The Psychology of Politics*, London: Routledge & Kegan Paul

Eysenck, H. J. (1956), 'The questionnaire measurement of neuroticism and extraversion', *Rev. di Psicol.,* **50**, 113–40

Eysenck, H. J. (1957a), *The Dynamics of Anxiety and Hysteria*, London: Routledge & Kegan Paul

Eysenck, H. J. (1957b), *Uses and Abuses of Psychology*, Harmondsworth: Penguin

Eysenck, H. J. (1959), 'The Rorschach test', in Buros (1959)

Eysenck, H. J. (1967), *The Biological Basis of Personality*, Springfield: C. C. Thomas

Eysenck, H. J. (1971), *Readings in Introversion–Extraversion II*, London: Staples Press

Eysenck, H. J. (1972), 'The experimental study of Freudian concepts', *Bull. Brit. Psychol. Soc.,* **25**, 261–8

Eysenck, H. J. (1976), 'The learning theory model of neurosis – a new approach', *Behav. Res. and Therap.,* **14**, 251–68

Eysenck, H. J., and Cookson, D. (1969), 'Personality in primary school children: 1, ability and achievement', *Brit. J. Educ. Psychol.,* **39**, 109–22

Eysenck, H. J., and Eysenck, S. B. G. (1964), *EPI Manual,* London: University of London Press

Eysenck, H. J., and Eysenck, S. B. G. (1969), *Personality Structure and Measurement,* London: Routledge & Kegan Paul

Eysenck, H. J., and Eysenck, S. B. G. (1975), *The EPQ,* London: University of London Press

Eysenck, H. J., and Eysenck, S. B. G. (1976), *Psychoticism as a Dimension of Personality,* London: Routledge & Kegan Paul

Eysenck, M. W., and Eysenck, H. J. (1980), 'Mischel and the concept of personality', *Brit. J. Psychol.,* **71**, 71–83

Eysenck, S. B. G., and Eysenck, H. J. (1968), 'The measurement of psychoticism. A study of factor stability and reliability', *Brit. J. Soc. Clin. Psychol.,* **7**, 286–94

Fallstrom, K., and Vegelius, J. (1976), 'A discriminatory analysis based on dichotomised Rorschach scores of diabetic children', unpublished ms., University of Göteborg

Fenichel, O. (1945), *The Psychoanalytic Theory of Neurosis,* New York: Norton

Ferguson, G. A. (1949), 'On the theory of test development', *Psychometrika,* **14**, 61–8

Fineman, S. (1977), 'The achievement motive construct and its measurement. Where are we now?', *Brit. J. Psychol.,* **68**, 1–22

Fiske, D. (1971), 'The analysis of tests and test-taking situations', in Cattell (1971a)

Fransella, F. (1980), 'Man as scientist', in A. Chapman and D. Jones (eds.), *Models of Man,* Leicester: BPS

French, J. W., Ekstrom, R. B., and Price, L. A. (1963), *Kit of Reference Tests for Cognitive Factors,* ETS Princeton

Freud, S. (1905), 'Three essays on sexuality', in *Collected Psychological Works of Sigmund Freud,* vol. 7, London: Hogarth Press and Institute of Psychoanalysis

Freud, S. (1908), 'Character and anal erotism', in *Collected Psychological Works of Sigmund Freud,* vol. 9, London: Hogarth Press and Institute of Psychoanalysis

Freud, S. (1920), 'Beyond the pleasure principle', in *Standard Edition of the Complete Psychological Works of Sigmund Freud* (1966), vol. 18, London: Hogarth Press and Institute of Psychoanalysis

Freud, S. (1924), 'Neurosis and psychosis', in *Standard Edition of the Complete Psychological Works of Sigmund Freud* (1966), vol. 19, London: Hogarth Press and Institute of Psychoanalysis

Fromm, E. (1974), *The Anatomy of Human Destructiveness*, London: Jonathan Cape

Glover, E. (1924), 'Notes on oral character formation', in E. Glover, *The Early Development of Mind* (1956), London: Mayo

Gough, H. G. (1965), *Adjective Check List*, Palo Alto: Consulting Psychologists Press

Gough, H. G. (1975), *Californian Psychological Inventory*, Palo Alto: Consulting Psychologists Press

Gray, H., and Wheelwright, J. B. (1946), 'Jung's psychological types: their frequency of occurrence', *J. Genetic Psychol.*, **34**, 3–17

Grygier, T. J. (1961), *The Dynamic Personality Inventory*, Windsor: NFER

Grygier, T. J. (1976), *The Dynamic Personality Inventory: Manual*, Windsor, NFER

Guilford, J. P. (1956), *Psychometric Methods*, New York: McGraw-Hill

Guilford, J. P. (1959), *Personality*, New York: McGraw-Hill

Guilford, J. P., and Hoepfner, R. (1971), *The Analysis of Intelligence*, New York: McGraw-Hill

Guilford, J. P., and Zimmerman, W. S. (1949), *The Guilford–Zimmerman Temperament Survey: Manual of instructions and interpretations*, Beverly Hills: Sheridan

Hakstian, A. R., and Cattell, R. B. (1974), 'The checking of primary ability structure on a broader base of performance', *Brit. J. Educ. Psychol.*, **44**, 140–54

Hakstian, A. R., and Muller, V. J. (1973), 'Some notes on the number of factors problem', *Multiv. Behav. Res.*, **8**, 461–75

Hall, C. S. (1934), 'Drive and emotionality: factors associated with adjustment in the rat', *J. Comp. Psychol.*, **17**, 89–108

Hall, C. S., and Lindzey, G. (1957), *Theories of Personality*, New York: Wiley

Hamilton, V. (1970), 'Non-cognitive factors in university students' performance', *Brit. J. Psychol.*, **61**, 229–41

Hampson, S. (1975), 'The personality characteristics of certain groups of mentally abnormal offenders', Ph.D thesis, University of Exeter

Hampson, S., and Kline, P. (1977), 'Personality dimensions differentiating certain groups of abnormal offenders from non-offenders', *Brit. J. Criminology*, **17**, 310–31

Harman, H. H. (1976), *Modern Factor Analysis*, 2nd edn, Chicago: University of Chicago Press

Harré, J. (1980), 'Man the rhetor', in A. Chapman and D. Jones (eds.), *Models of Man*, Leicester: BPS

Hartshorne, H., and May, M. A. (1928), *Studies in Deceit*, New York: Macmillan

Hartshorne, H., and May, M. A. (1929), *Studies in Service and Self Control*, New York: Macmillan

Hathaway, S. R., and McKinley, J. C. (1961), *The Minnesota Multiphasic Personality Inventory Manual* (revised), New York: Psychological Corporation

Heim, A. W. (1975), *Psychological Testing*, London: Oxford University Press

Helmes, E. (1980), 'A psychometric investigation of the Eysenck personality questionnaire', *Appl. Psychol. Meas.*, **4**, 43–55

Hentschel, V., Schubo, W., and Zerssen, D. V. (1976), 'Attempts at a nosological classification with two standardised psychiatric rating scales', *Ach. Psychiat. Nemenkr.*, **221**, 283–301

Hinde, R. A. (1966), *Animal Behaviour*, Cambridge: Cambridge University Press

Hogan, R. (1978), 'The personality research form', in Buros (1978)

Hogan, R., De Suto, C. B., and Solano, C. (1977), 'Traits, tests and personality research', *Amer. Psychol.*, **32**, 4, 255–64

Holley, J. W. (1973), 'Rorschach analysis', in Kline (1973b)

Holley, J. W. (1975), 'Some comments on the design of experimental studies in clinical research', *Psychol. Res. Bull.*, **15**, 10 (Lund: University of Lund)

Holley, J. W., and Guilford, J. P. (1964), 'A note on the G index of agreement', *Educ. Psychol. Meas.*, **24**, 749–53

Holley, J. W., and Nilsson, I. K. (1973), 'On the validity of some clinical measures', *Psychol. Res. Bull.*, **13**, 4 (Lund: University of Lund)

Holtzman, W. H. (1968) 'Holtzman inkblot technique', in Rabin (1968)

Honess, T., and Kline, P. (1974a), 'Extraversion, neuroticism and academic performance in Uganda', *Brit. J. Educ. Psychol.*, **45**, 44–6

Honess, T., and Kline, P. (1974b), 'The use of the EPI and the JEPI with a student population in Uganda', *Brit. J. Soc. Clin. Psychol.*, **13**, 96–8

Howarth, E. (1976), 'Were Cattell's "personality sphere" factors correctly identified in the first instance?' *Brit. J. Psychol.*, **67**, 2, 213–30

Howarth, E. (1980), *Howarth Personality Questionnaire*, Alberta: University of Alberta Press

Howarth, E., and Schockman-Gates, Kar-Lá (1980), 'Self-report multiple mood instruments', *Brit J. Psychol.* (in press)

Hoyt, C. (1941), 'Test reliability obtained by analysis of variance', *Psychom.*, **6**, 153–60

Hull, C. L. (1943), *Principles of Behaviour*, New York: Appleton-Century-Crofts

Hundal, P. S. (1970), 'Achievement motivation of fast and slow progressing entrepreneurs measured by projective techniques', in *Rorschach Proceedings VII*, Berne: Hans Huber

Hundleby, J. (1973), 'The measurement of personality by objective tests', in Kline (1973b)

Jackson, D. N. (1974), *Personality Research Form*, New York: Research Psychol. Press

James, W. (1890), *Principles of Psychology*, New York: Holt

Jonsson, H. (1975), 'A factorial study of schizophrenia', *Scand. J. Psychol.,* **16**, 125–30

Jonsson, H., and Franzen, G. (1976), 'Evaluation of some factor-analytically derived sub-classes of schizophrenia', *Psychol. Res. Bull.,* **16**, 1 (Lund: University of Lund)

Jung, C. G. (1923), *Psychological Types*, New York: Harcourt Brace

Kaiser, H. F. (1958), 'The varimax criterion for analytic rotation in factor analysis', *Psychometrika,* **23**, 187–200

Katkin, E. S. (1978), 'The State–Trait Anxiety Inventory', in Buros (1978)

Kelly, G. A. (1955), *The Psychology of Personal Constructs*, vols. 1 and 2, New York: Norton

Kiesler, D. J. (1966), 'Some myths of psychotherapy research and the research for a paradigm', *Psychol. Bull.,* **65**, 110–36

Klein, M. (1948), *Contributions to Psychoanalysis*, London: Hogarth Press

Kleinsmith, L. J., and Kaplan, S. (1963), 'Paired associate learning as a function of arousal and interpolated interval', *J. Exp. Psychol.,* **65**, 190–3

Kleinsmith, L. J., and Kaplan, S. (1964), 'Interaction of arousal and recall interval in nonsense-syllable paired associate learning', *J. Exp. Psychol.,* **67**, 124–6

Kline, P. (1966a), 'Extraversion, neuroticism and academic performance among Ghanaian university students', *Brit. J. Educ. Psychol.,* **36**, 93–4

Kline, P. (1966b), 'Obsessional traits, obsessional symptoms and anal erotism', *Brit. J. Med. Psychol.,* **41**, 299–305

Kline, P. (1967), 'Obsessional traits and emotional instability in a normal population', *Brit. J. Med. Psychol.,* **40**, 193–7

Kline, P. (1968), 'The validity of the Dynamic Personality Inventory', *Brit. J. Med. Psychol.,* **41**, 307–11

Kline, P. (1969), 'The anal character: a cross-cultural study in Ghana', *Brit. J. Soc. Clin. Psychol.,* **8**, 201–10

Kline, P. (1971), *Ai3Q Test*, Windsor: NFER

Kline, P. (1972), *Fact and Fantasy in Freudian Theory*, 1st edn, London: Methuen

Kline, P. (1973a), 'Assessment in psychodynamic psychology', in Kline (1973b)

Kline, P. (ed.) (1973b), *New Approaches in Psychological Measurement*, Chichester: Wiley

Kline, P. (1975), *The Psychology of Vocational Guidance*, London: Batsford

Kline, P. (1977), 'Personality and learning', in M. J. A. Howe (ed.), *Adult Learning*, Chichester: Wiley

Kline, P. (1978), 'The status of the anal character: a methodological and empirical reply to Holmes', *Brit. J. Med. Psychol.,* **51**, 87–90

Kline, P. (1979), *Psychometrics and Psychology,* London: Academic Press

Kline, P. (1980a), *OOQ and OPQ Personality Tests* (handbook), Windsor: NFER

Kline, P. (1980b), *OOQ and OPQ Tests,* Windsor: NFER

Kline, P. (1980c), 'Percept-genetic theory and technique', *Brit. J. Projective Psychol,* **25**, 7–12

Kline, P. (1980d), 'The Psychometric Model of Man', in A. Chapman and D. Jones (eds.), *Models of Man,* Leicester: BPS

Kline, P. (1981), *Fact and Fantasy in Freudian Theory,* 2nd edn, London: Methuen

Kline, P. (1982), *The Construction of Psychological Tests* (in preparation)

Kline, P., and Cooper, C. (1977), 'A percept-genetic study of some defence mechanisms in the test PN', *Scand. J. Psychol.,* **18**, 148–52

Kline, P., and Gale, A. M. (1971), 'Extraversion, neuroticism and performance in a psychology examination', *Brit. J. Educ. Psychol.,* **41**, 90–3

Kline, P., and Grindley, J. (1974), 'A 28-day case-study with the MAT', *J. Mult. Exper. Personl. Clin. Psychol.,* **1**, 13–32

Kline, P., and Storey, R. (1977), 'A factor analytic study of the oral character', *Brit. J. Soc. Clin. Psychol.,* **16**, 317–28

Kline, P., and Storey, R. (1978), 'The dynamic personality: what does it measure?', *Brit. J. Psychol.,* **68**, 375–83

Kline, P., and Storey, R. (1980), 'The aetiology of the oral character', *J. Genetic Psychol.,* **136**, 85–94

Kline, P., and Svaste-Xuto, B. (1981), 'The HTP Test in Thailand', *Brit. J. Project. Psychol.,* **26**, 1–11

Klopfer, B., *et al.* (1956), *Developments in the Rorschach Technique,* vol. 2, *Fields of Application,* New York: Harcourt Brace

Kragh, U. (1955), *The Actual Genetic Model of Perception Personality,* Lund: Gleerup

Kragh, U. (1969), *The Defence Mechanism Test,* Stockholm: Testförlaget

Kragh, U., and Smith, G. (1970), *Percept-Genetic Analysis,* Lund: Gleerup

Krout, M. H., and Tabin, J. K. (1954), 'Measuring personality in developmental terms', *Genet. Psychol. Monogr.,* **50**, 289–335

Kuder, G. F. (1970), *Kuder General Interest Survey,* Chicago: Science Research Associates

Lacey, J. I. (1967), 'Somatic response patterning and stress: some revisions of activation theory', in Appley and Trumbull (1967)

Lee, S. G. (1963), *Manual of a Thematic Apperception Test for African Subjects,* Pietermaritzburg: University of Natal Press

Levonian, E. (1961), 'Personality measurement with items selected from the 16PF questionnaire', *Educ. Psychol. Meas.,* **21**, 937–46

Levy, P. (1973), 'On the relation between test theory and psychology', in Kline (1973b)

Loo, R. (1979), 'A psychometric investigation of the Eysenck Personality Questionnaire', *J. Personal. Assess.*, **43**, 54–8

Lord, F. M. (1974), *Individualised Testing and Item Characteristic Curve Theory*, ETS Princeton

Lord, F. M., and Novick, M. R. (1968), *Statistical Theories of Mental Test Scores*, New York: Addison-Wesley

Lykken, D. T. (1972), 'The Clyde Mood Scale', in Buros (1972)

Lynn, R. (1969), 'An achievement motivation questionnaire', *Brit. J. Psychol.*, **60**, 4, 529–34

McClelland, D. C. (1961), *The Achieving Society*, Princeton: Van Nostrand

McDougall, W. (1932), *Energies of Men*, London: Methuen

Madan, V. (1967), 'The relation of neuroticism and extraversion to intelligence and educational attainment at different age levels', Ph.D thesis, University of Punjab, Chandigarh

Magnussen, D., and Endler, N. S. (eds.) (1977), *Personality at the Crossroads: Current Issues in Interactional Psychology*, Hillsdale: Erlbaum

Mayer-Gross, W., Slater, E., and Roth, M. (1967), *Clinical Psychiatry*, London: Cassell

Meehl, P. E. (1954), *Clinical vs. Statistical Prediction*, Minnesota: University of Minnesota Press

Mischel, W. (1968), *Personality and Assessment*, New York: Wiley

Mischel, W. (1973), 'Towards a cognitive social learning reconceptualisation of personality', *Psychol. Rev.*, **80**, 4, 252–83

Mischel, W. (1977a), 'On the future of personality measurement', *Amer. Psychol.*, **32**, 4, 246–54

Mischel, W. (1977b), 'The interaction of person and situation', in Magnussen and Endler (1977)

Mohan, V., and Kumar, D. (1976), 'Quantitative analysis of the performance of introverts and extraverts on standard progressive matrices', *Brit. J. Psychol.*, **67**, 391–8

Mowrer, O. H. (1950), *Learning Theory and Personality Dynamics*, New York: Ronald

Murray, H. A. (1938), *Explorations in Personality*, New York: Oxford University Press

Murstein, B. I. (1963), *Theory and Research in Projective Techniques*, New York: Wiley

Nesselroade, J. R., and Baltes, P. B. (1975), 'Higher-order convergence of two distinct personality systems: Cattell's HSPQ and Jackson's PRF', *Mult. Behav. Res.*, **10**, 387–408

Nowlis, V., and Nowlis, H. H. (1956), 'The description and analysis of mood', *Anals. New York Acad. Sci.*, **65**, 345–55

Nunnally, J. (1978), *Psychometric Theory*, New York: McGraw-Hill

Orne, M. T. (1962), 'On the social psychology of the psychological experiment', *Amer. Psychol.*, **17**, 776–83

Osgood, C. E., Suci, G. J., and Tannenbaum, P. M. (1957), *The Measurement of Meaning*, Illinois: University of Illinois Press

Pawlik, K., and Cattell, R. B. (1964), 'Third-order factors in objective personality tests', *Brit. J. Psychol.*, **55**, 1–18

Pervin, A. L. (1975), *Personality Theory Assessment and Research*, New York: Wiley

Plutchik, R. (1966), 'Multiple rating scales for the measurement of affective states', *J. Clin. Psychol.*, **22**, 423–5

Popper, K. (1959), *The Logic of Scientific Discovery*, New York: Basic Books

Price-Williams, P. R. (ed.) (1965), *Cross-Cultural Studies*, Harmondsworth: Penguin

Rabin, A. I. (ed.) (1968), *Projective Techniques in Personality Assessment*, New York: Springer

Rasch, G. (1960), *Probabilistic Models for some Intelligence and Attainment Tests*, Copenhagen: Danish Institute for Pedagogy

Rasch, G. (1961), 'On general laws and the meaning of measurement in psychology', in *Proceedings of the Fourth Berkeley Symposium on Mathematical Statistics and Probability*, vol. 4, Berkeley: University of California Press

Rasch, G. (1966), 'An item-analysis which takes individual differences into account', *Brit. J. Math. Stat. Psychol.*, **19**, 49–57

Reid, R. L. (1960), 'Inhibition – Pavlov, Hull, Eysenck', *Brit. J. Psychol.*, **51**, 226–36

Richardson, M. W., and Kuder, G. F. (1939), 'The calculation of test reliability coefficients based on the method of rational equivalence', *J. Educ. Psychol.*, **30**, 681–7

Rokeach, M. (1960), *The Open and Closed Mind*, New York: Basic Books

Rorschach, H. (1921), *Psychodiagnostics*, Berne: Hans Huber

Rosenzweig, S. (1951), 'Idiodynamics in personality theory with special reference to projective methods', *Psychol. Rev.*, **58**, 213–23

Sarason, S. B. (1972), *Personality: An Objective Approach*, New York: Wiley

Saville, P., and Blinkhorn, S. (1976), *Undergraduate Personality by Factored Scales*, Windsor: NFER

Schneider, K. (1958), *Psychopathic Personalities*, London: Cassell

Schonell, F. J. (1944), *Backwardness in the Basic Subjects*, Edinburgh: Oliver & Boyd

Schubo, W., Hentschel, V., Zerssen, D. V., and Mombour, W. (1975), 'Psychiatric classification by means of a discriminatory application of Q factor-analysis', *Arch. Psychiat. Nervenkr.*, **220**, 187–200

Semeonoff, B. (1973), 'New developments in projective testing', in Kline (1973b)

Semeonoff, B. (1977), *Projective Tests*, Chichester: Wiley

Shouksmith, G. (1968), *Assessment through Interviewing,* Oxford: Pergamon

Sjoback, H. (1967), *Defence Mechanism Test*, Lund: Colytographic Research Foundation

Skinner, B. F. (1953), *Science and Human Behaviour*, New York: Macmillan

Slater, P. (1964), *The Principal Components of a Repertory Grid*, London: Vincent Andrews

Spielberger, C. B., Gorsuch, P. L., and Lustene, R. E. (1970), *State–Trait Anxiety Inventory*, Palo Alto: Consulting Psychologists Press

Strong, E. K., Campbell, D. P., Berdie, R. E., and Clerk, K. E. (1971), *Strong Vocational Interest Blank*, Stanford: Stanford University Press

Thurstone, L. L. (1947), *Multiple Factor Analysis: A Development and Expansion of Vectors of the Mind*, Chicago: Chicago University Press

Vagy, P. R., and Hammond, S. B. (1976), 'The number and kind of invariant personality Q factors: a partial replication of Eysenck and Eysenck', *Brit. J. Soc. Clin. Psychol.*, **15**, 121–30

Vegelius, J. (1976), 'On various G index generalisations and their applicability within the clinical domain', Uppsala: *Acta Univ. Uppsaliensis*

Velicer, W. F. (1976), 'Determining the number of components from the matrix of partial correlations', *Psychometrika,* **41**, 321–7

Vernon, P. E. (1964), *Personality Assessment*, London: Methuen

Vernon, P. E., and Parry, J. B. (1949), *Personnel Selection in the British Forces*, London: University of London Press

Warburton, F. W. (1968), 'The structure of personality factors', Unpublished ms., University of Manchester

Westerlundh, B. (1976), *Aggression, Anxiety and Defence*, Lund: Gleerup

Willet, T. C. (1964), *Criminal on the Road*, London: Tavistock

Wilson, G. D., and Patterson, J. R. (1970), *The Conservatism Scale*, Windsor: NFER

Witkin, H. A. (1962), *Psychological Differentiation: Studies of Development,* New York: Wiley

Wood, R. (1978), 'Fitting the Rasch model – a heady tale', *Brit. J. Math. Stat. Psychol.,* **31**, 27–32

Zubin, J., Eron, L. D., and Schumer, F. (1966), *An Experimental Approach to Projective Techniques*, London: Wiley

Index